Third Grade Math with Confidence

Student Workbook

Part B

Third Grade Math with Confidence

Student Workbook
Part B

KATE SNOW

WELL-TRAINED MIND PRESS

Names: Snow, Kate (Teacher), author.

Title: Third grade math with confidence. Student workbook part B / Kate Snow.

Other titles: Student workbook part B

Description: [Charles City, Virginia] : Well-Trained Mind Press, [2023] | Series: Math with confidence | Interest age level: 007-009.

Identifiers: ISBN: 978-1-944481-31-5 (paperback)

Subjects: LCSH: Mathematics--Study and teaching (Elementary) | LCGFT: Problems and exercises. | BISAC: JUVENILE NONFICTION / MATHEMATICS / Arithmetic.

Classification: LCC: QA107.2 .S663 2023 | DDC: 372.7--dc23

Reprinted May 2024 by Mercury Print Productions

4 5 6 7 8 9 10 11 Mercury 30 29 28 27 26 25 24

Table of Contents

Author's Note

You'll need three books to teach *Third Grade Math with Confidence*. All three books are essential for the program.

- The Instructor Guide contains the scripted lesson plans for the entire year (Units 1-16).
- Student Workbook Part A contains the workbook pages for the first half of the year (Units 1-8).
- Student Workbook Part B contains the workbook pages for the second half of the year (Units 9-16).

The Student Workbooks are not meant to be used as stand-alone workbooks. The hands-on teaching activities in the Instructor Guide are an essential part of the program. You'll need the directions in the Instructor Guide to guide your child through the Lesson Activities pages. The icon with two heads means that your child should complete these pages with you, and that she is not expected to complete these pages on her own.

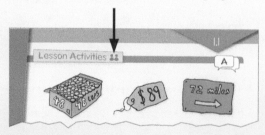

The Practice and Review pages give your child practice with new concepts and review previously-learned skills. The icon with one head means that your child may complete these pages on his own. Most third-graders will be able to complete these workbook pages independently, but some may need help reading and interpreting the directions.

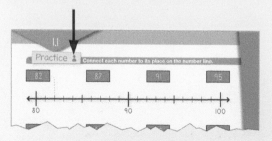 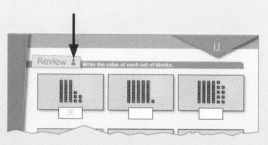

Lesson Activities 👥

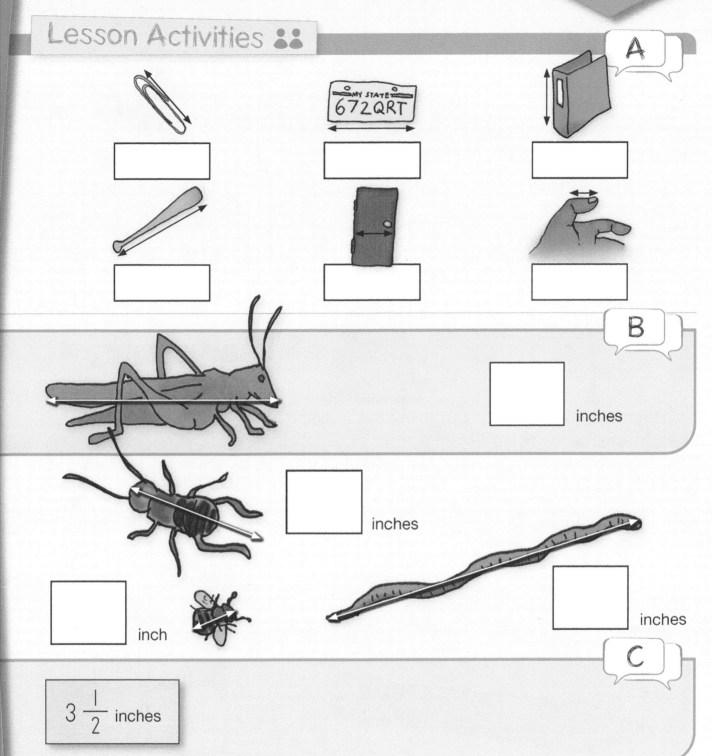

inches

inches

inch

inches

$3 \frac{1}{2}$ inches

$2 \frac{1}{2}$ inches

$4 \frac{1}{2}$ inches

Practice

Circle the more sensible measurement for each item.

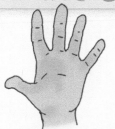

Width of your hand

| 5 inches | 5 feet |

Distance between cities

| 100 yards | 100 miles |

Length of a river

| 150 miles | 150 feet |

Height of a flagpole

| 35 feet | 35 inches |

Length of a swimming pool

| 25 yards | 25 miles |

Length of a pencil

| 7 inches | 7 feet |

Use a ruler to measure the school supplies to the nearest half-inch.

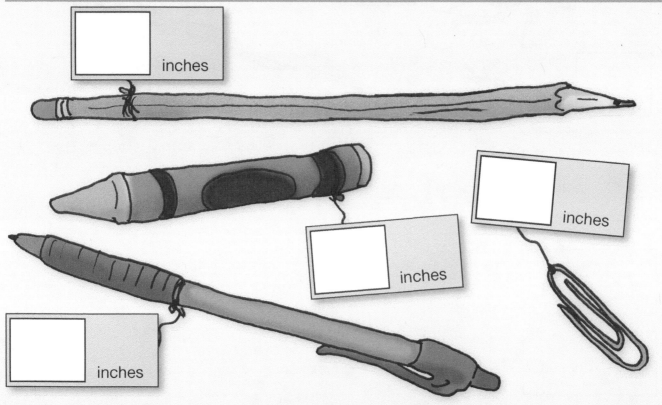

[____] inches

[____] inches

[____] inches

[____] inches

Review   Complete.

	6
×	8

	8
×	7

	9
×	6

	7
×	6

	1 0
×	9

	8
×	9

	7
×	7

	8
×	8

	6
×	6

	1 0
×	1 0

Write the time.

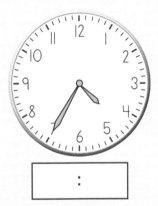

| : |

| : |

| : |

| : |

Solve. Write the equations you use.

Calvin packed 9 bags of pretzels for a picnic. He put 7 pretzels in each bag. How many pretzels did he use?

Cora bought cocoa mix for $3.59 and marshmallows for $1.79. How much did she spend?

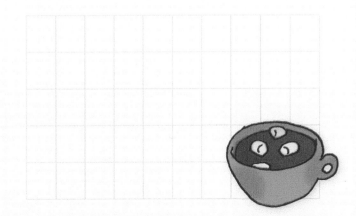

Lesson Activities 👥

Unit	inch	foot	yard	mile
Abbreviation	in.	ft.	yd.	mi.

in.

in.

in.

in.

in.

	Height (in.)	Width (in.)
Book 1		
Book 2		
Book 3		

Practice 👤 Use a ruler to measure the sticks to the nearest quarter-inch.

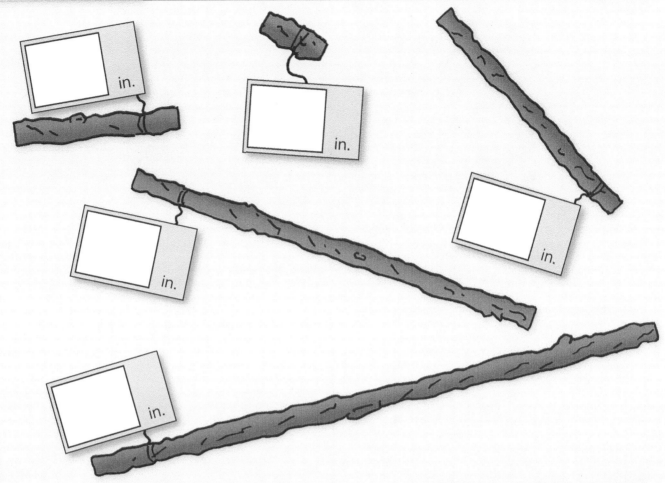

in.

in.

in.

in.

in.

Use a ruler to draw a line that matches each length.

$2 \frac{1}{4}$ in.

$2 \frac{3}{4}$ in.

$3 \frac{1}{2}$ in.

4 in.

$4 \frac{3}{4}$ in.

Review 👤 Complete the multiplication chart.

×	5	6	7	8	9	10
5	25	30	35	40	45	50
6	30					60
7	35					70
8	40					80
9	45					90
10	50	60	70	80	90	100

Wesley asked his friends and family about their favorite winter activities. Use the chart to complete the bar graph.

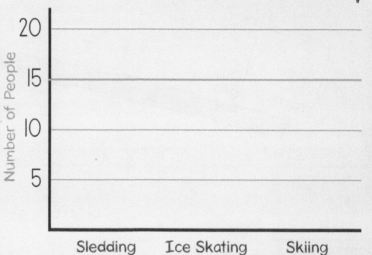

Activity	Number of People
Sledding	17
Ice Skating	12
Skiing	6

Favorite Winter Activity

Complete.

94 − 36 = ☐

58 + 27 = ☐

75 − 68 = ☐

90 + 40 = ☐

30 × 4 = ☐

80 × 6 = ☐

50 × 7 = ☐

9 × 40 = ☐

Lesson Activities

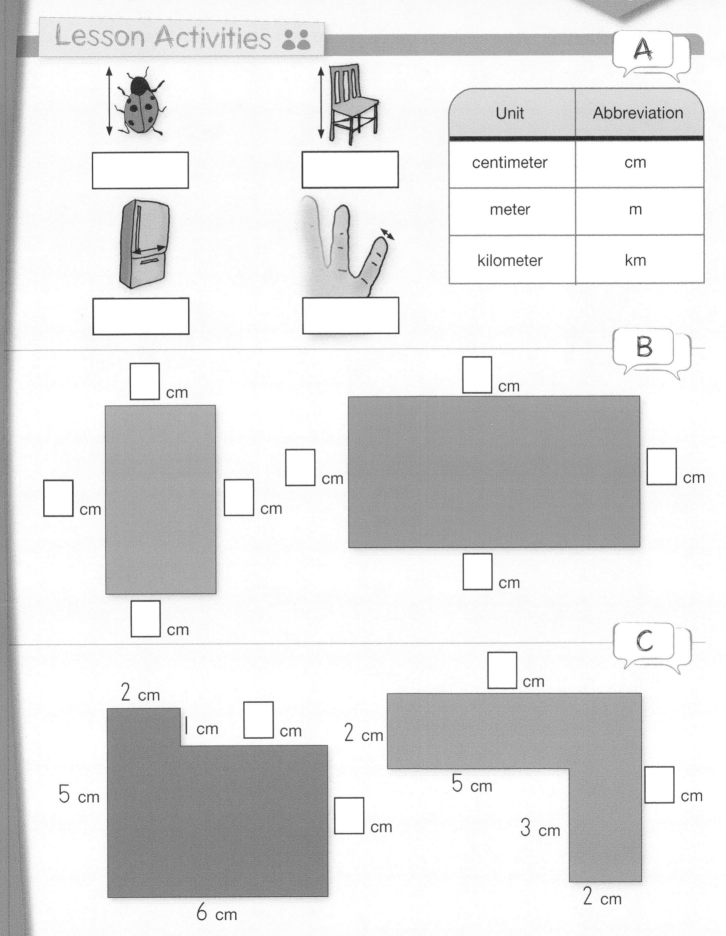

Unit	Abbreviation
centimeter	cm
meter	m
kilometer	km

A

B

C

☐ cm

☐ cm
☐ cm

☐ cm
☐ cm

☐ cm

☐ cm
☐ cm

☐ cm

2 cm
1 cm   ☐ cm

5 cm

☐ cm

6 cm

☐ cm

2 cm

5 cm

☐ cm

3 cm

2 cm

Practice

Circle the more sensible measurement for each item.

Distance between cities

| 100 meters | 100 kilometers |

Height of an elephant

| 3 meters | 3 kilometers |

Length of a worm

| 10 meters | 10 centimeters |

Height of a book

| 25 centimeters | 25 meters |

Length of a hike

| 6 meters | 6 kilometers |

Length of a bus

| 11 meters | 11 centimeters |

Use logical thinking to label the missing sides of the shapes.

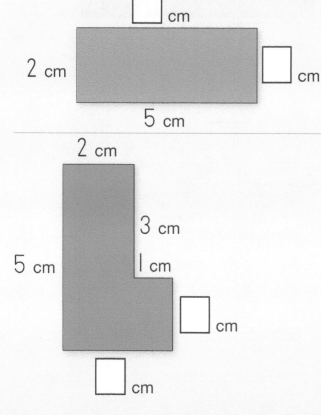

☐ cm

2 cm

5 cm

☐ cm

6 cm

☐ cm

1 cm

☐ cm

2 cm

3 cm

1 cm

5 cm

☐ cm

☐ cm

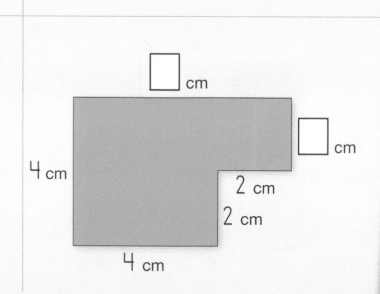

☐ cm

4 cm

☐ cm

2 cm

2 cm

4 cm

Review 👤 Use a ruler to draw a line that matches each length.

$2\dfrac{1}{2}$ in.

$3\dfrac{3}{4}$ in.

Complete the sequences.

Count by 100s
| | | | 600 | 700 | | | |

Count by 50s
| | | | 650 | 700 | | | |

Count by 25s
| | | | 675 | 700 | | | |

Complete.

```
  7 . 4 2
- 3 . 0 8
_____
$
```

```
  5 . 3 8
+ 2 . 9 9
_____
$
```

Complete.

```
      6
×     7
```

```
      8
×     6
```

```
      7
×     8
```

```
      7
×     9
```

```
      6
×     9
```

```
      9
×     9
```

Lesson Activities

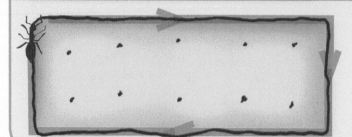

Perimeter

The distance around the outside edge

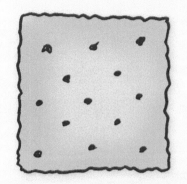

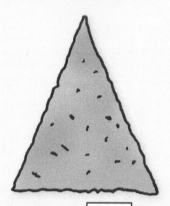

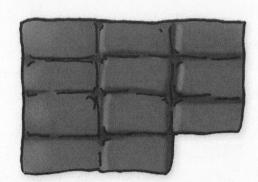

Perimeter: ☐ cm

Perimeter: ☐ cm

Perimeter: ☐ cm

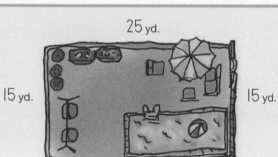

25 yd.

15 yd.   15 yd.

25 yd.

What is the perimeter of the yard?

12 in.

18 in.   18 in.

12 in.

Perimeter: ☐ in.

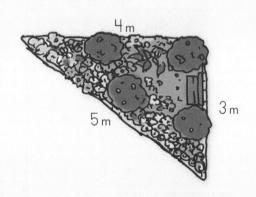

4 m

5 m   3 m

Perimeter: ☐ m

C

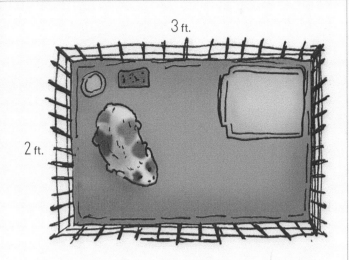

3 ft.

2 ft.

Perimeter: [ ] ft.

Fun Run Course

start and End

1 km

1 km

2 km

1 km

Bayside Park

Perimeter: [ ] km

Practice Find the perimeter of each shape.

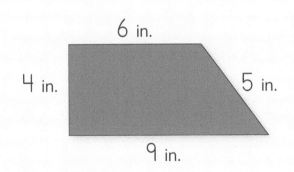

6 in.

4 in.

5 in.

9 in.

Perimeter: [ ] in.

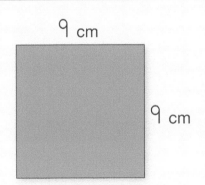

9 cm

9 cm

Perimeter: [ ] cm

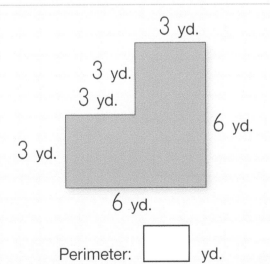

3 yd.

3 yd.

3 yd.

6 yd.

3 yd.

6 yd.

Perimeter: [ ] yd.

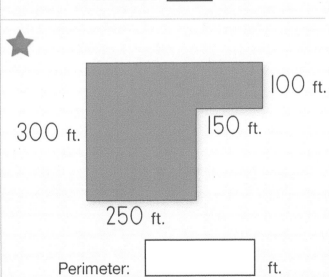

⭐

100 ft.

300 ft.

150 ft.

250 ft.

Perimeter: [ ] ft.

Review   Circle the more sensible measurement for each item.

Length of an aquarium

1 yard	1 mile

Height of a cereal box

13 inches	13 yards

Length of a bathtub

5 yards	5 feet

Complete.

$$\frac{6}{8} - \frac{1}{8} = \boxed{\frac{}{}}$$

$$\frac{2}{6} + \frac{3}{6} = \boxed{\frac{}{}}$$

$$\frac{2}{4} + \frac{1}{4} = \boxed{\frac{}{}}$$

$$\frac{2}{3} - \frac{1}{3} = \boxed{\frac{}{}}$$

Complete.

$3 \times 5 + 4 = \boxed{}$

$6 \times 2 + 1 = \boxed{}$

$10 \times 5 + 4 = \boxed{}$

$8 \times 4 + 2 = \boxed{}$

$5 \times 5 + 3 = \boxed{}$

Match.

6×8	45
8×7	48
9×6	49
7×7	54
9×5	56

Lesson Activities 👥

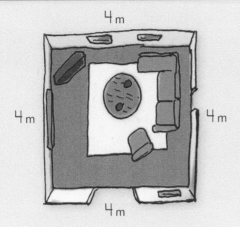

4 m

4 m 4 m

4 m

What is the perimeter of the room?

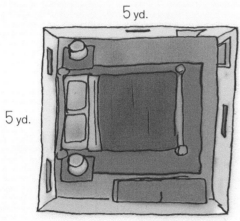

5 yd.

5 yd.

Perimeter: ☐ yd.

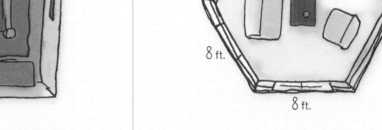

8 ft.

8 ft. 8 ft.

8 ft. 8 ft.

8 ft.

Perimeter: ☐ ft.

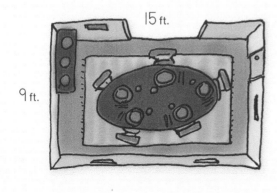

15 ft.

9 ft.

Perimeter: ☐ ft.

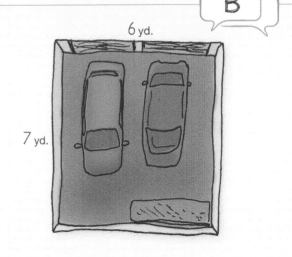

6 yd.

7 yd.

Perimeter: ☐ yd.

Lesson 9.5

13

Practice 👤 **Find the perimeter of each shape.**

All sides are 20 yd. long.

Perimeter: ☐ yd.

All sides are 5 ft. long.

Perimeter: ☐ ft.

All sides are 9 cm long.

Perimeter: ☐ cm

⭐ All sides are 2 in. long.

Perimeter: ☐ in.

3 cm

5 cm

Perimeter: ☐ cm

3 km

1 km

Perimeter: ☐ km

12 in.   12 in.

20 in.   20 in.

Perimeter: ☐ in.

20 in.

12 in.   12 in.

20 in.

Perimeter: ☐ in.

Review   Circle the more sensible unit for each item.

Length of a fork

| 20 centimeters | 20 meters |

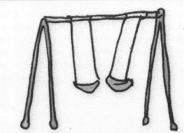

Length of a playground

| 50 meters | 50 kilometers |

Length of a baby

| 50 meters | 50 centimeters |

Complete.

2 weeks = ☐ days

4 weeks = ☐ days

5 weeks = ☐ days

6 weeks = ☐ days

9 weeks = ☐ days

Match.

9 × 7		56
9 × 8		63
8 × 7		64
9 × 9		72
8 × 8		81

Solve. Write the equations you use.

A box of chocolates costs $6.29.
A box of valentines costs $1.35 less than a box of chocolates.
How much does a box of valentines cost?

Marco played outside for 60 minutes. He spent 15 minutes making a snowman, 20 minutes building a snow fort, and the rest of the time throwing snowballs. How much time did he spend throwing snowballs?

Lesson Activities 👥

Kaya made a poster 20 inches long and 15 inches wide. What is the perimeter of the poster?

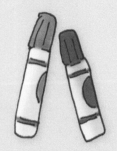

Ja'shon helps his parents build a chicken coop with 6 sides. Each side is 4 feet long. What is the perimeter of the chicken coop?

Kelsey and her dad use 30 feet of fence to enclose this garden. How long is the shortest side of the garden?

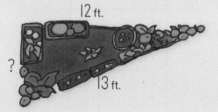

12 ft.
?
13 ft.

Jonah's yard has a perimeter of 115 meters. How long is the unlabeled side of the yard?

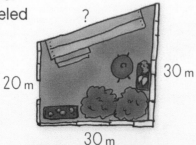

?
20 m
30 m
30 m

Practice 👤 Solve. Write the equations you use.

Caroline's bedroom is shaped like a rectangle. It is 12 feet long and 10 feet wide. What is the perimeter of her bedroom?

Zayne used craft sticks to make a pentagon with 5 sides. Each craft stick is 4 inches long. What is the perimeter of the pentagon?

The perimeter of this triangle is 20 meters. How long is the unlabeled side?

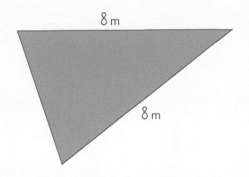

8 m

8 m

 Lucas built this rectangle with blocks. The perimeter of the rectangle is 54 inches. The longer sides are 15 inches long. How long are the shorter sides?

15 in.

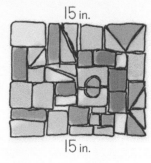

15 in.

Review 👤 Connect each number to its dot on the number line.

| 507 | 525 | 548 | 589 | 593 |

| 505 | 558 | 570 | 599 | 582 |

Complete.

$9.01 = \boxed{}$ ¢

$5.75 = \boxed{}$ ¢

$\boxed{}$ = 250 ¢

$\boxed{}$ = 800 ¢

Round to the nearest dollar.

$9.78	
$0.95	
$6.07	
$4.55	

Match.

6 × 7		42
9 × 7		56
8 × 8		63
7 × 8		64

8 × 9		48
7 × 7		49
9 × 9		72
8 × 6		81

Lesson Activities 👥

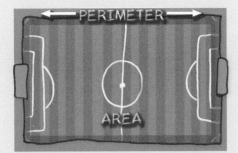

A

Perimeter
The distance around
the outside edge of a shape

Area
The amount of space
the shape covers.

B

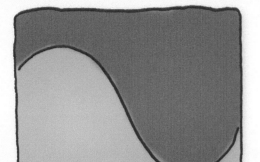

Perimeter: ☐ cm

Area: ☐ square cm

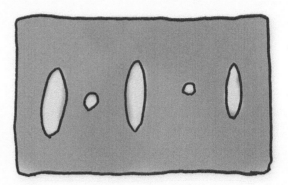

Perimeter: ☐ cm

Area: ☐ square cm

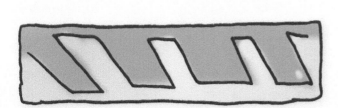

Perimeter: ☐ cm

Area: ☐ square cm

Perimeter: ☐ cm

Area: ☐ square cm

Practice 🧍 Find the perimeter and area of each shape.

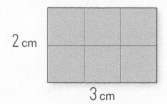

2 cm

3 cm

Perimeter: ☐ cm

Area: ☐ square cm

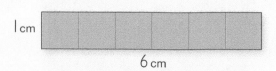

1 cm

6 cm

Perimeter: ☐ cm

Area: ☐ square cm

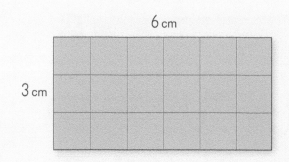

6 cm

3 cm

Perimeter: ☐ cm

Area: ☐ square cm

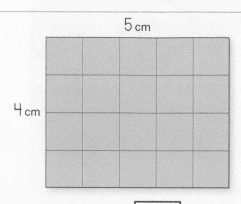

5 cm

4 cm

Perimeter: ☐ cm

Area: ☐ square cm

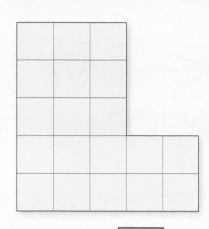

Perimeter: ☐ cm

Area: ☐ square cm

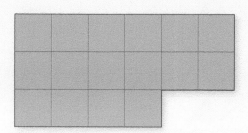

Perimeter: ☐ cm

Area: ☐ square cm

Review

Use a ruler to measure the straws to the nearest quarter-inch.

in.

in.

in.

Complete.

5 weeks, 1 day = ☐ days

4 weeks, 2 days = ☐ days

5 weeks, 5 days = ☐ days

10 weeks, 3 days = ☐ days

Match.

8 × 8		36
6 × 6		49
9 × 9		64
10 × 10		81
7 × 7		100

Solve. Write the equations you use.

Madelyn organized her stuffed animals. She has 3 shelves, and she put 7 animals on each shelf. She had 2 stuffed animals left, so she put them on her bed. How many stuffed animals does she have?

The chocolate chip cookie box has 4 rows of 9 cookies. The lemon cookie box has 6 rows of 7 cookies. How many cookies are there in all?

Lesson Activities 👥

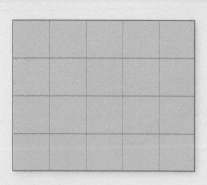

Perimeter: ☐ cm

Area: ☐ sq. cm

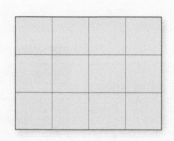

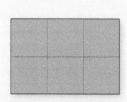

Perimeter: ☐ cm   Perimeter: ☐ cm   Perimeter: ☐ cm

Area: ☐ sq. cm   Area: ☐ sq. cm   Area: ☐ sq. cm

B

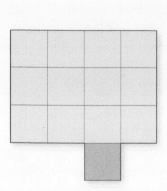

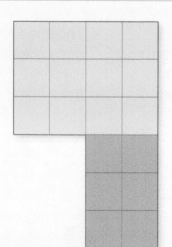

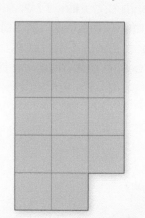

Area: ☐ sq. cm   Area: ☐ sq. cm   Area: ☐ sq. cm

Practice 👤 **Find the area of each shape.**

☐ sq. cm

☐ sq. cm

☐ sq. cm

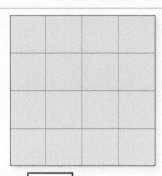

☐ sq. cm

☐ sq. cm

☐ sq. cm

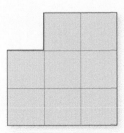

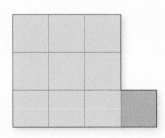

☐ sq. cm

☐ sq. cm

☐ sq. cm

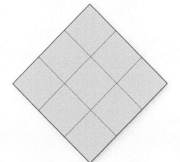

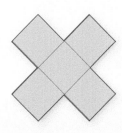

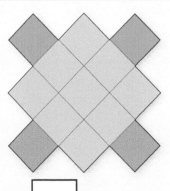

☐ sq. cm

☐ sq. cm

☐ sq. cm

Review

Use the pictograph to answer the questions.
Write a multiplication equation to match each question.

Ryan's Hockey Practice

Tuesday | \ \ \ \ \
Thursday | \ \ \ \
Saturday | \ \ \ \

\ = 20 minutes

How many minutes did Ryan practice on Tuesday?

How many minutes did Ryan practice on Thursday?

How many minutes did Ryan practice on Saturday?

Complete.

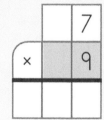

```
  6 4 6
- 2 0 9
```

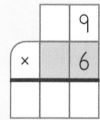

```
  4 3 1
+ 5 6 9
```

Complete.

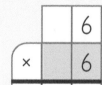

```
      7
  ×   9
```

```
      6
  ×   6
```

```
      4
  ×   8
```

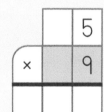

```
      9
  ×   6
```

```
      5
  ×   9
```

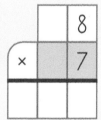

```
      8
  ×   7
```

Solve. Write the equations you use.

Aaron has $37.
He buys 4 books.
Each book costs $8.
How much money
does he have left?

Lesson Activities 👥

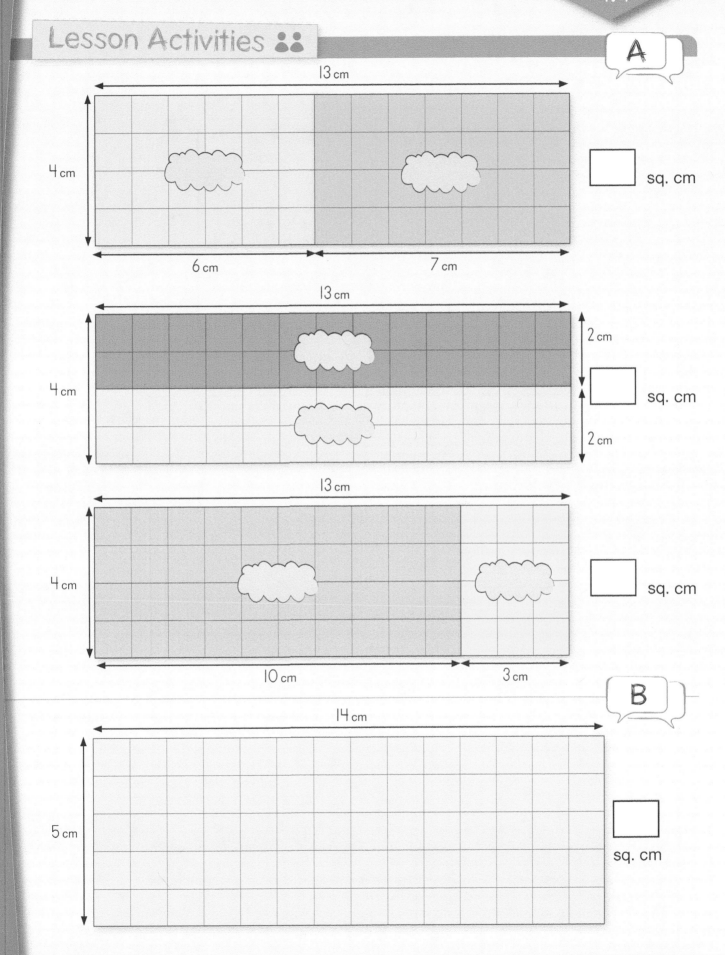

13 cm

4 cm

6 cm   7 cm

☐ sq. cm

13 cm

4 cm

2 cm

2 cm

☐ sq. cm

13 cm

4 cm

10 cm   3 cm

☐ sq. cm

14 cm

5 cm

☐ sq. cm

Practice 👤 Split each rectangle into smaller rectangles.
Then, find the area of the whole rectangle.
The first rectangle has already been split for you.

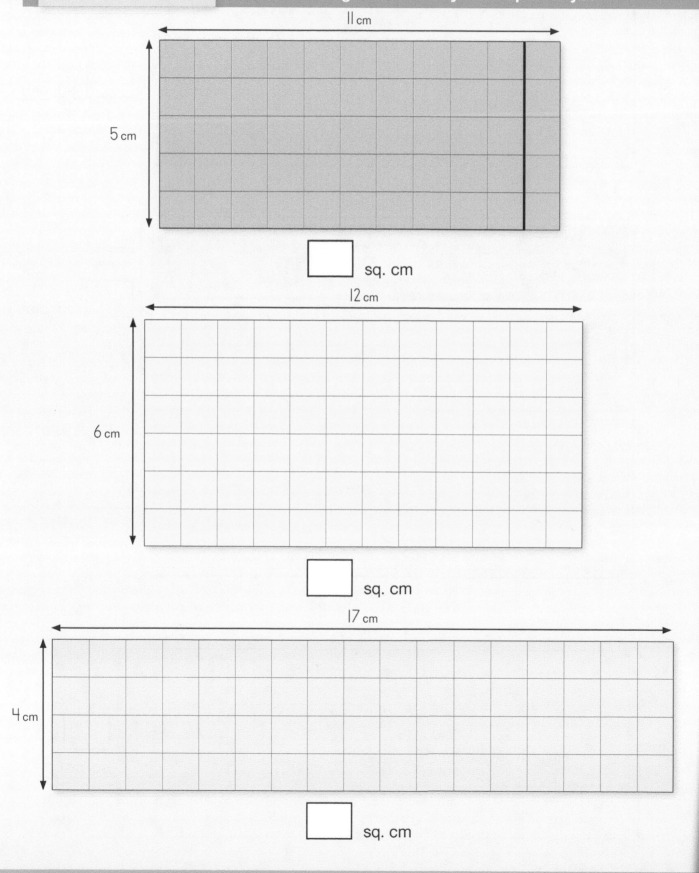

11 cm

5 cm

☐ sq. cm

12 cm

6 cm

☐ sq. cm

17 cm

4 cm

☐ sq. cm

Review 👤 Choose the more sensible unit for each item.

Height of a mug

| 4 feet | 4 inches |

Height of a door

| 8 feet | 8 inches |

Height of a tree

| 20 yards | 20 miles |

Complete.

$7 \times 6 + 1 = \boxed{}$

$8 \times 8 + 2 = \boxed{}$

$9 \times 7 + 7 = \boxed{}$

$6 \times 8 + 2 = \boxed{}$

$7 \times 8 + 5 = \boxed{}$

Complete.

$47 + \boxed{} = 52$

$\boxed{} + 6 = 77$

$100 - \boxed{} = 55$

$\boxed{} - 12 = 48$

$40 - \boxed{} = 2$

Solve. Write the equations you use.

 The dinosaur costs $1.35 less than the yo-yo. The deck of cards costs $0.79 more than the dinosaur. How much does the deck of cards cost?

$5.79

Lesson Activities

1 cm

1 cm

1 square centimeter
(sq. cm)

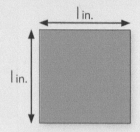

1 in.

1 in.

1 square inch
(sq. in.)

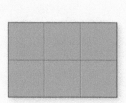

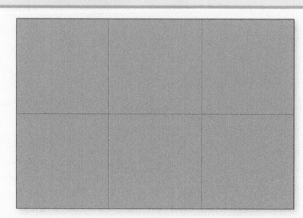

Area: _____

Area: _____

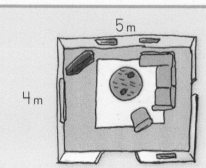

5 m

4 m

What is the area of the room?

6 in.

8 in.

Area: _____

4 yd.

3 yd.

Area: _____

Practice

Use the grid lines to find the area of each shape.
Circle the correct units.

sq. in.
sq. cm

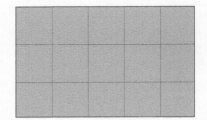

sq. in.
sq. cm

Find the area of each item.

5 m

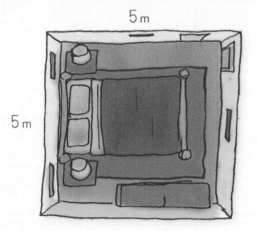

5 m

Area:

12 ft.

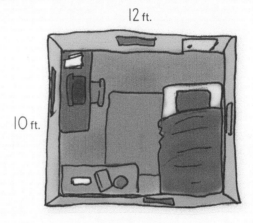

10 ft.

Area:

10 in.

13 in.

Area:

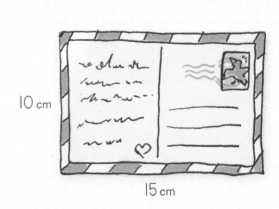

10 cm

15 cm

Area:

Review

Circle the more sensible measurement for each item.

Height of a mug

10 centimeters	10 meters

Height of a door

2 centimeters	2 meters

Height of a tree

20 meters	20 kilometers

Complete.

$3 \times 4 =$ ☐ $7 \times 8 =$ ☐ $2 \times 9 =$ ☐

$6 \times 9 =$ ☐ $8 \times 4 =$ ☐ $8 \times 3 =$ ☐

$4 \times 5 =$ ☐ $8 \times 8 =$ ☐ $9 \times 4 =$ ☐

$0 \times 7 =$ ☐ $7 \times 3 =$ ☐ $9 \times 9 =$ ☐

$9 \times 3 =$ ☐ $7 \times 9 =$ ☐ $6 \times 4 =$ ☐

Solve. Write the equations you use.

Mark's book is 319 pages long. Vera's book is 278 pages long. How many pages longer is Mark's book than Vera's?

Mark's book is 319 pages long. Vera's book is 278 pages long. How many pages are in both books?

Lesson Activities 👥

Serafina made a poster 10 inches long and 6 inches wide. What is the area of the poster?

Jeffrey helped his dad plant sod in a square part of the yard. Each side of the square was 8 feet long. How many square feet did they cover?

The shorter side of the rug is 6 feet long. The other side is 4 feet longer. What is the area of the rug?

6 ft.

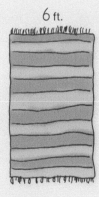

The longer side of the pool is 5 meters long. The other side is 1 meter shorter. What is the area of the pool?

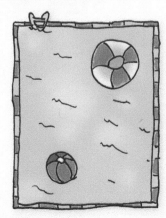

5 m

Practice 👤 Solve. Write the equations you use.

Caroline's bedroom is shaped like a rectangle. It is 12 feet long and 10 feet wide. What is the area of her bedroom?

Zayne used 4 craft sticks to make a square. Each craft stick is 5 inches long. What is the area of the square?

The shorter side of the pool is 4 yards long. The other side is 3 yards longer. What is the area of the pool?

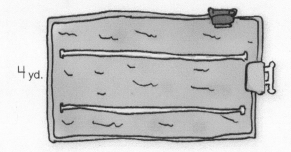

4 yd.

⭐ The perimeter of this garden bed is 14 feet. What is its area?

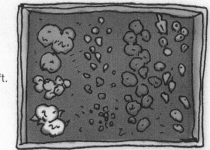

3 ft.

Review

Use the numbers to complete the blanks.
You will use each number once.

| 1 | 2 | 3 | 4 | 5 | 6 | 7 | 8 | 9 |

$\square \times 8 = 16$ $3 \times \square = 12$ $10 \times \square = 90$

$\square \times 4 = 20$ $6 \times \square = 18$ $3 \times \square = 24$

$\square \times 5 = 35$ $10 \times \square = 60$ $17 \times \square = 17$

Complete.

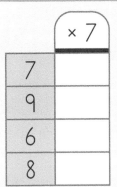

× 7	
7	
9	
6	
8	

× 8	
6	
8	
9	
7	

× 9	
9	
7	
8	
6	

Copy the shapes.

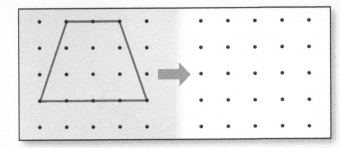

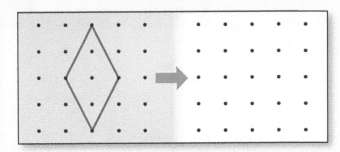

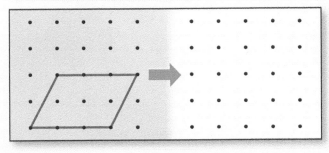

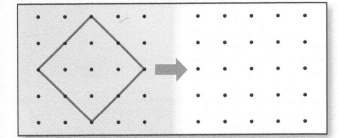

Unit Wrap-Up

Use a ruler to measure the sticks to the nearest quarter-inch.

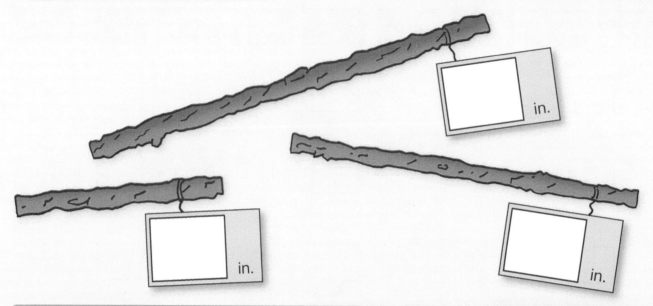

in.

in.

in.

Circle the more sensible unit for each item.

Area of a rug

| 40 sq. ft. | 40 sq. in. |

Area of a sticky note

| 25 sq. cm | 25 sq. m |

Area of a parking lot

| 300 sq. m | 300 sq. km |

Find the perimeter. Include the correct unit.

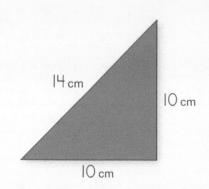

14 cm

10 cm

10 cm

Perimeter: _____

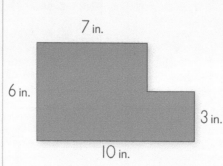

7 in.

6 in.

3 in.

10 in.

Perimeter: _____

All sides are 6 m.

Perimeter: _____

34

Unit Wrap-Up

Find the area. Include the correct unit.

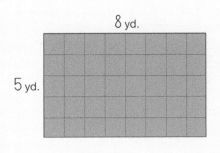

8 yd.

5 yd.

Area: [   ]

5 cm

6 cm

Area: [   ]

3 in.

5 in.

2 in.

6 in.

Area: [   ]

Split the rectangle into smaller rectangles. Then, find the area of the whole rectangle.

13 cm

5 cm

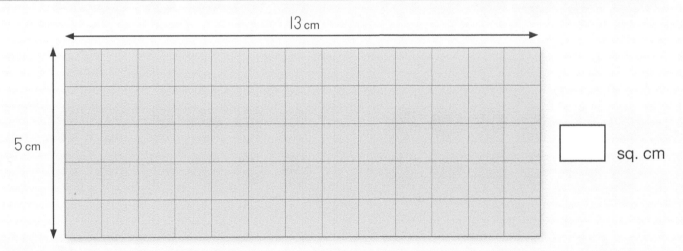

[   ] sq. cm

Solve. Write the equations you use.

Hannah's kitchen is 20 ft. long and 18 ft. wide. What is the perimeter of the kitchen?

The shorter side of the sandbox is 8 ft. long. The other side is 2 ft. longer.
What is the perimeter of the sandbox?

8 ft.

Lesson Activities

A

Multiplication

$3 \times 4 = 12$

number of   size of   total
groups   each group

Division

$12 \div 3 = 4$

total   number of   size of
groups   each group

$12 \div 6 = \boxed{}$

$12 \div 2 = \boxed{}$

$12 \div 4 = \boxed{}$

$12 \div 12 = \boxed{}$

B

Total Number of Cookies	Number of People	Division Equation
6	3	
10	2	
10	5	
0	4	
15	15	

Practice

Complete. Draw rings around the crackers to show how you divided them.

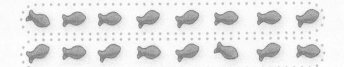

Split 16 into 2 equal groups.
How many are in each group?

16 ÷ 2 = ☐

Split 16 into 8 equal groups.
How many are in each group?

16 ÷ 8 = ☐

16 ÷ 4 = ☐

16 ÷ 16 = ☐

18 ÷ 3 = ☐

18 ÷ 6 = ☐

18 ÷ 9 = ☐

18 ÷ 2 = ☐

Review Complete the sequences.

Count by 50s: 950, 1,000

Count by 25s: 975, 1,000

Count by 20s: 980, 1,000

Find the perimeter and area of each rectangle.

7 in.

5 in.

Perimeter:

Area:

5 ft.

10 ft.

Perimeter:

Area:

Complete.

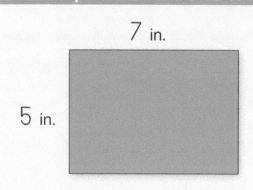

	Half
20	
10	
18	
14	
16	

Complete.

8 × 7 = ☐   9 × 6 = ☐

5 × 9 = ☐   8 × 4 = ☐

6 × 6 = ☐   7 × 7 = ☐

8 × 9 = ☐   8 × 8 = ☐

Lesson Activities

You have 14 cookies.
You split them equally with your brother.
How many do each of you get?

$14 \div 2 = \boxed{}$

Half of 14 is $\boxed{}$.

$16 \div 2 = \boxed{}$ $20 \div 2 = \boxed{}$ $8 \div 2 = \boxed{}$

$10 \div 2 = \boxed{}$ $6 \div 2 = \boxed{}$ $4 \div 2 = \boxed{}$

$2 \div 2 = \boxed{}$ $18 \div 2 = \boxed{}$ $12 \div 2 = \boxed{}$

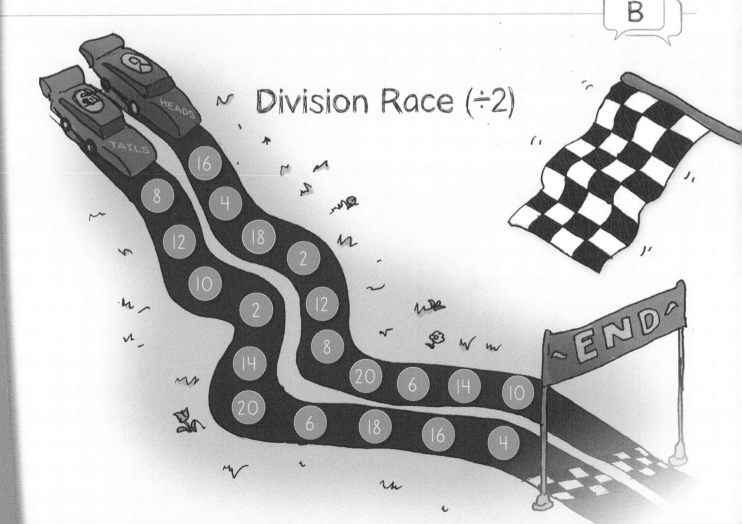

Division Race (÷2)

Practice 👤 Complete.

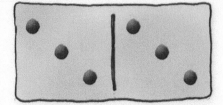

6 ÷ 2 = ☐

10 ÷ 2 = ☐

16 ÷ 2 = ☐

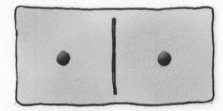

2 ÷ 2 = ☐

14 ÷ 2 = ☐

12 ÷ 2 = ☐

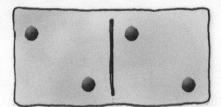

4 ÷ 2 = ☐

18 ÷ 2 = ☐

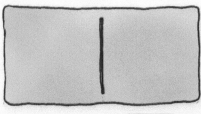

10 ÷ 2 = ☐

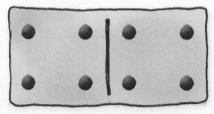

8 ÷ 2 = ☐

Review   Find the area of each shape.

 sq. cm

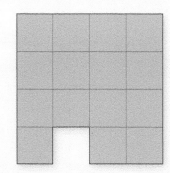
 sq. cm

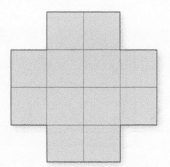
[ ] sq. cm

Complete the fact family.

$$\boxed{7} + \boxed{9} = \boxed{16}$$

$$\boxed{} + \boxed{} = \boxed{}$$

$$\boxed{} - \boxed{} = \boxed{}$$

$$\boxed{} - \boxed{} = \boxed{}$$

Complete.

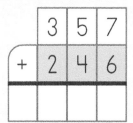

	3	5	7
+	2	4	6

	3	1	2
−	1	7	5

Solve. Write the equations you use.

Sarah has $23.
She buys 2 craft kits.
Each craft kit costs $10.
How much money does
she have left?

Liam buys yarn for $5.39
and a crochet hook for $2.74.
How much does he spend?

Lesson Activities

☐ × ☐ = ☐

☐ × ☐ = ☐

☐ ÷ ☐ = ☐

☐ ÷ ☐ = ☐

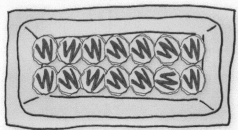

☐ × ☐ = ☐

☐ × ☐ = ☐

☐ ÷ ☐ = ☐

☐ ÷ ☐ = ☐

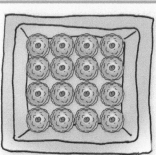

☐ × ☐ = ☐

☐ ÷ ☐ = ☐

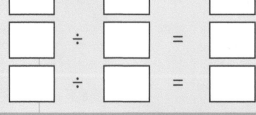

$18 ÷ 3 =$ ☐

$3 × ☐ = 18$

$20 ÷ 5 =$ ☐

$5 × ☐ = 20$

$30 ÷ 3 =$ ☐

$3 × ☐ = 30$

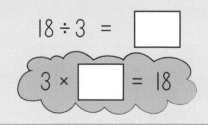

$12 ÷ 4 =$ ☐

$4 × ☐ = 12$

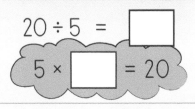

$21 ÷ 3 =$ ☐

$3 × ☐ = 21$

Practice

Complete the fact families to match the arrays.

$$2 \times 9 = 18$$
$$\boxed{} \times \boxed{} = \boxed{}$$
$$\boxed{} \div \boxed{} = \boxed{}$$
$$\boxed{} \div \boxed{} = \boxed{}$$

$$\boxed{} \times \boxed{} = \boxed{}$$
$$\boxed{} \times \boxed{} = \boxed{}$$
$$\boxed{} \div \boxed{} = \boxed{}$$
$$\boxed{} \div \boxed{} = \boxed{}$$

Complete the equations to match the arrays.

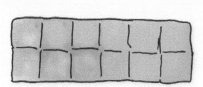

$$2 \times \boxed{} = 12$$
$$12 \div 2 = \boxed{}$$

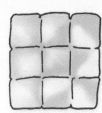

$$3 \times \boxed{} = 9$$
$$9 \div 3 = \boxed{}$$

$$5 \times \boxed{} = 25$$
$$25 \div 5 = \boxed{}$$

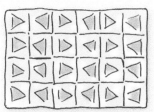

$$4 \times \boxed{} = 24$$
$$24 \div 4 = \boxed{}$$

10.3

Use the grid lines to find the area of each shape. Circle the correct units.

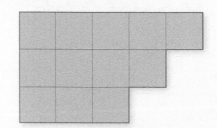

⬜ sq. in.
sq. cm

⬜ sq. in.
sq. cm

Write the multiples in order.

Multiples of 8 → | 8 | 16 | 24 | | | | | | | 80 |

Multiples of 9 → | 9 | 18 | | | | | | | | 90 |

Round to the nearest hundred.

373	692	817	436	501	760

Complete.

593 +10 ⬜ +10 ⬜ +10 ⬜ +10 633

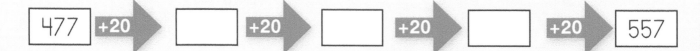

477 +20 ⬜ +20 ⬜ +20 ⬜ +20 557

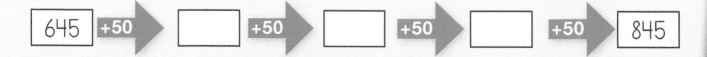

645 +50 ⬜ +50 ⬜ +50 ⬜ +50 845

Lesson Activities 👥

A

12 children split into groups of 2.
How many groups do they make?

12 ÷ 2 = ☐

total   size of   number of
         each group   groups

12 ÷ 4 = ☐

12 ÷ 6 = ☐

12 ÷ 3 = ☐

12 ÷ 12 = ☐

B

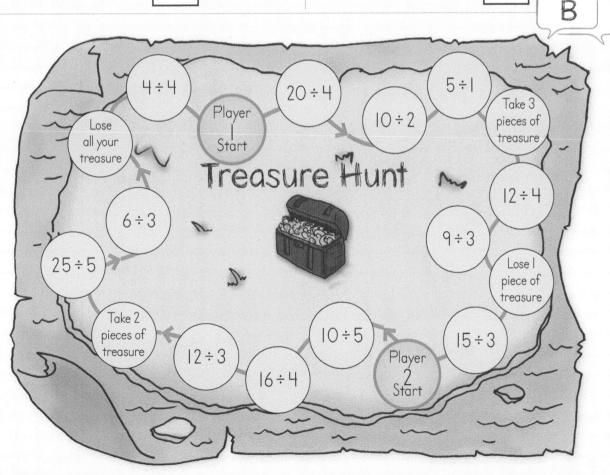

Practice Complete. Draw rings around the candies
to show how you divided them.

How many groups of 2 equal 16?

16 ÷ 2 = [8]

How many groups of 8 equal 16?

16 ÷ 8 = [ ]

How many groups of 4 equal 16?

16 ÷ 4 = [ ]

How many groups of 16 equal 16?

16 ÷ 16 = [ ]

How many groups of 3 equal 18?

18 ÷ 3 = [ ]

How many groups of 6 equal 18?

18 ÷ 6 = [ ]

How many groups of 9 equal 18?

18 ÷ 9 = [ ]

How many groups of 2 equal 18?

18 ÷ 2 = [ ]

Review 👤   **Choose the more sensible unit for each item.**

Area of a bulletin board

6 sq. ft.	6 sq. in.

Area of a zoo

1 sq. mi.	1 sq. yd.

Area of a book's cover

54 sq. ft.	54 sq. in.

Match.

$2.50 + $3.25		$6.00 - $2.50
	$5.75	
$1.50 + $2.50		$6.00 - $1.75
	$3.50	
$2.75 + $0.75		$6.00 - $0.25
	$4.00	
$1.75 + $2.50		$6.00 - $2.00
	$4.25	

Complete.

1 minute = ☐ seconds

1 hour = ☐ minutes

1 day = ☐ hours

1 week = ☐ days

Complete.

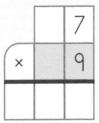

	7
×	9

	9
×	9

	1	0
×	1	0

	7
×	8

	7
×	5

	6
×	7

10.5

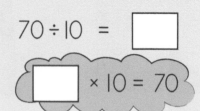

A

$70 \div 10 = \boxed{}$

$\boxed{} \times 10 = 70$

$90 \div 10 = \boxed{}$ $40 \div 10 = \boxed{}$ $60 \div 10 = \boxed{}$

$30 \div 10 = \boxed{}$ $10 \div 10 = \boxed{}$ $100 \div 10 = \boxed{}$

$50 \div 10 = \boxed{}$ $20 \div 10 = \boxed{}$ $80 \div 10 = \boxed{}$

B

Four in a Row

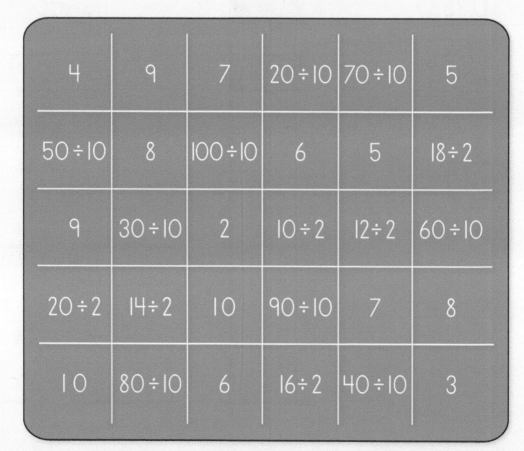

4	9	7	$20 \div 10$	$70 \div 10$	5
$50 \div 10$	8	$100 \div 10$	6	5	$18 \div 2$
9	$30 \div 10$	2	$10 \div 2$	$12 \div 2$	$60 \div 10$
$20 \div 2$	$14 \div 2$	10	$90 \div 10$	7	8
10	$80 \div 10$	6	$16 \div 2$	$40 \div 10$	3

Practice 👤 | Match.

40 ÷ 10	3	10 ÷ 2
30 ÷ 10	4	8 ÷ 2
60 ÷ 10	5	12 ÷ 2
80 ÷ 10	6	6 ÷ 2
90 ÷ 10	7	18 ÷ 2
50 ÷ 10	8	20 ÷ 2
100 ÷ 10	9	14 ÷ 2
70 ÷ 10	10	16 ÷ 2

Solve. Write a division equation to match.

There are 14 children.
They split into 2 equal teams.
How many children are on each team?

You have 30 flowers.
You put 10 flowers in
each vase. How many
vases do you fill?

☐ ÷ ☐ = ☐   ☐ ÷ ☐ = ☐

Review   Find the perimeter and area.

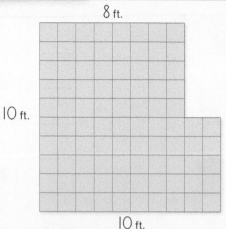

8 ft.

10 ft.

5 ft.

10 ft.

Perimeter: [＿＿＿＿＿＿]

Area: [＿＿＿＿＿＿]

Complete the sequences.

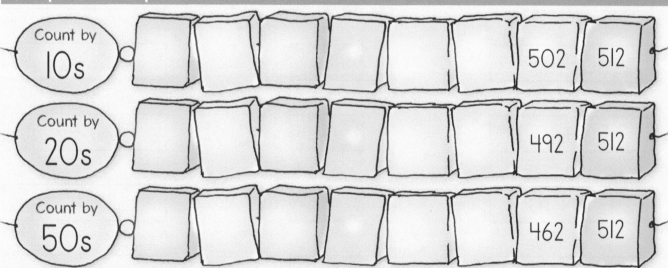

Count by 10s   □ □ □ □ □ □ 502 512

Count by 20s   □ □ □ □ □ □ 492 512

Count by 50s   □ □ □ □ □ □ 462 512

Complete.

2 weeks, 4 days = □ days

4 weeks, 1 day = □ days

8 weeks, 2 days = □ days

7 weeks, 3 days = □ days

★ 11 weeks = □ days

Copy the shapes.

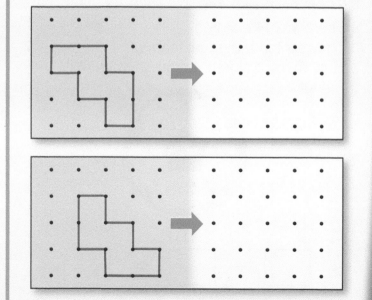

Lesson Activities 👥

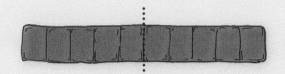
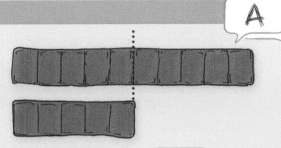

$10 \div 5 =$ ☐

$15 \div 5 =$ ☐

$20 \div 5 =$ ☐

$25 \div 5 =$ ☐

$30 \div 5 =$ ☐

$35 \div 5 =$ ☐

$40 \div 5 =$ ☐

$45 \div 5 =$ ☐

B

SPIN AND COVER

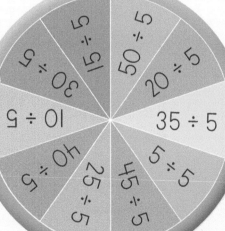

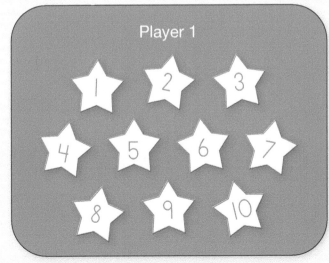

Player 1

Player 2

Practice   Complete.

$20 \div 5 = \boxed{}$

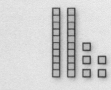

$25 \div 5 = \boxed{}$

$10 \div 5 = \boxed{}$

$15 \div 5 = \boxed{}$

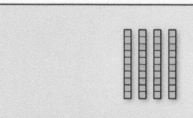

$40 \div 5 = \boxed{}$

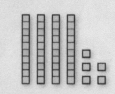

$45 \div 5 = \boxed{}$

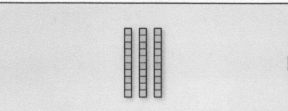

$30 \div 5 = \boxed{}$

$35 \div 5 = \boxed{}$

★ $100 \div 5 = \boxed{}$ ➡ ★ $105 \div 5 = \boxed{}$

Review

Circle the more sensible unit for each item.

Area of a cellphone screen

100 sq. m	100 sq. cm

Area of a rug

3 sq. m	3 sq. km

Area of a zoo

2 sq. m	2 sq. km

Complete.

$

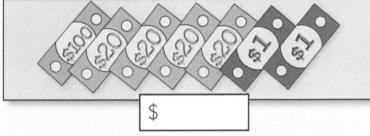

$

Complete.

$6 \times 8 =$ ☐

$4 \times 7 =$ ☐

$8 \times 7 =$ ☐

$9 \times 4 =$ ☐

$7 \times 7 =$ ☐

Solve. Write the equations you use.

Noah made a square quilt. Each side is 3 feet long. What is the perimeter of the quilt?

Noah made a square quilt. Each side is 3 feet long. What is the area of the quilt?

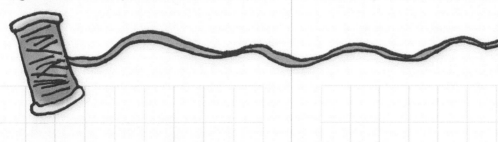

Lesson Activities 👥

Division Crash (÷5)

15 ÷ 5	25 ÷ 5	40 ÷ 5	10 ÷ 5	35 ÷ 5
45 ÷ 5	20 ÷ 5	5 ÷ 5	30 ÷ 5	50 ÷ 5

$$8 ÷ 2 = 4$$
dividend   divisor   quotient

C

5 friends equally share 20 lollipops.
How many lollipops does each friend get?

You have 20 lollipops.
You put 5 lollipops in each goodie bag.
How many goodie bags do you make?

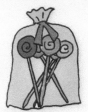

You need 80 markers.
How many packs should you buy?

You have 16 feet of rope.
You cut it into 2 equal pieces.
How long is each piece?

Practice 👤 Complete.

☐ × 5 = 20	20 ÷ 5 = ☐
☐ × 5 = 40	40 ÷ 5 = ☐
☐ × 5 = 25	25 ÷ 5 = ☐
☐ × 5 = 35	35 ÷ 5 = ☐
☐ × 5 = 45	45 ÷ 5 = ☐
☐ × 5 = 30	30 ÷ 5 = ☐
☐ × 5 = 50	50 ÷ 5 = ☐

Solve. Write a division problem to match.

There are 10 doughnuts in each box.
You need 50 doughnuts.
How many boxes should you buy?

You have 20 inches of ribbon. You need
5 inches of ribbon for each bookmark.
How many bookmarks can you make?

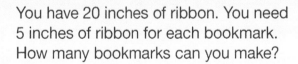

20 inches

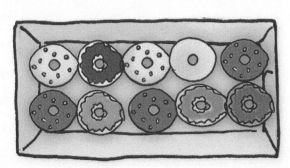

☐ ÷ ☐ = ☐   ☐ ÷ ☐ = ☐

10.7

Split the rectangle into smaller rectangles. Then, find the area of the whole rectangle.

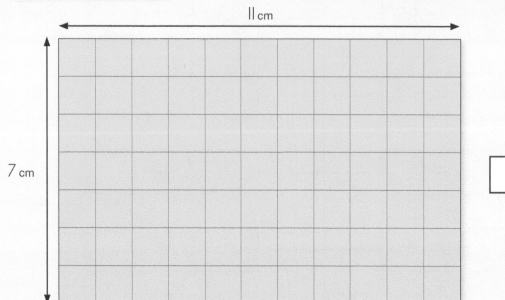

11 cm

7 cm

☐ sq. cm

Complete the fact family.

| 3 | × | 7 | = | 21 |

| 7 | × | ☐ | = | ☐ |

| 21 | ÷ | ☐ | = | ☐ |

| 21 | ÷ | ☐ | = | ☐ |

Complete.

$10 \times 4 + 6 =$ ☐

$9 \times 5 + 3 =$ ☐

$2 \times 9 + 1 =$ ☐

$6 \times 5 + 3 =$ ☐

Use a ruler to measure each line to the nearest quarter-inch.

inches

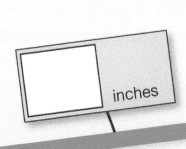

inches

Lesson Activities 👥

A

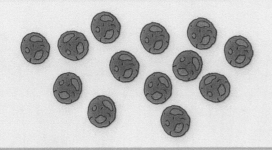 13 ÷ 4 = ☐

 11 ÷ 2 = ☐    10 ÷ 3 = ☐

 12 ÷ 5 = ☐   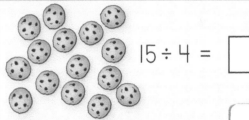 15 ÷ 4 = ☐

B

Roll and Divide

Player 1	Player 2
14 ÷ ☐ = ☐	14 ÷ ☐ = ☐
8 ÷ ☐ = ☐	8 ÷ ☐ = ☐
9 ÷ ☐ = ☐	9 ÷ ☐ = ☐
16 ÷ ☐ = ☐	16 ÷ ☐ = ☐
21 ÷ ☐ = ☐	21 ÷ ☐ = ☐
Sum of remainders ☐	Sum of remainders ☐

Practice 👤 Complete.

16 ÷ 5 = ☐

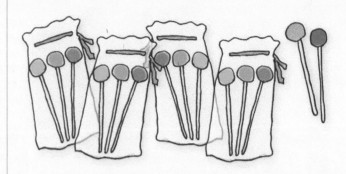

14 ÷ 3 = ☐

23 ÷ 4 = ☐

23 ÷ 6 = ☐

34 ÷ 10 = ☐

34 ÷ 5 = ☐

Review

Complete.

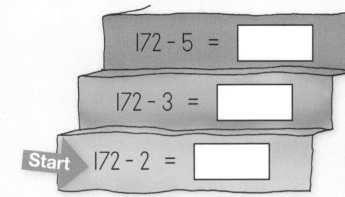

172 − 5 = ☐

172 − 3 = ☐

Start 172 − 2 = ☐

299 + 14 = ☐

299 + 4 = ☐

299 + 1 = ☐

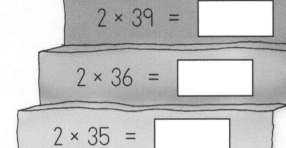

2 × 39 = ☐

2 × 36 = ☐

2 × 35 = ☐

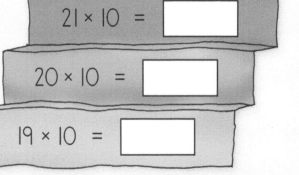

21 × 10 = ☐

20 × 10 = ☐

19 × 10 = ☐

Complete.

	Half
60	
64	
70	
72	
76	

Complete.

4 × 4 = ☐   6 × 7 = ☐

9 × 5 = ☐   5 × 6 = ☐

8 × 1 = ☐   8 × 8 = ☐

9 × 7 = ☐   6 × 4 = ☐

Color the odd numbers red. Color the even numbers pink.

898   98   9   988   899   89   8   989   809

Unit Wrap-Up 👤 **Complete.**

12 ÷ 3 = ☐

18 ÷ 2 = ☐

7 ÷ 7 = ☐

10 ÷ 5 = ☐

Complete the fact family to match the array.

☐ × ☐ = ☐

☐ × ☐ = ☐

☐ ÷ ☐ = ☐

☐ ÷ ☐ = ☐

Use the words in the word bank to complete the sentences.

24 is the _____.

4 is the _____.

6 is the _____.

> divisor
>
> ○
>
> quotient
>
> ○
>
> dividend

Unit Wrap-Up 👤

Complete.

20 ÷ 5 = ☐   90 ÷ 10 = ☐   16 ÷ 2 = ☐

30 ÷ 10 = ☐   25 ÷ 5 = ☐   15 ÷ 5 = ☐

10 ÷ 1 = ☐   20 ÷ 2 = ☐   50 ÷ 5 = ☐

45 ÷ 5 = ☐   40 ÷ 10 = ☐   14 ÷ 2 = ☐

18 ÷ 2 = ☐   35 ÷ 5 = ☐   70 ÷ 10 = ☐

Complete.

19 ÷ 5 = ☐   19 ÷ 2 = ☐   19 ÷ 10 = ☐

Solve. Write the equations you use.

30 children are at swim lessons. They divide into groups with 10 children in each group. How many groups do they make?

☐ ÷ ☐ = ☐

Maya sets up 15 chairs. She arranges them in rows of 5. How many rows does she make?

☐ ÷ ☐ = ☐

Lesson Activities

Base-ten Blocks

Money

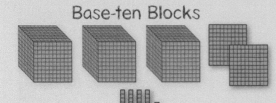

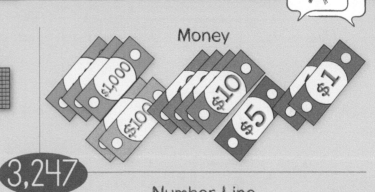

3,247

Expanded Form

Number Line

$3,000 + 200 + 40 + 7$

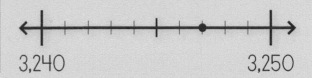

3,240   3,250

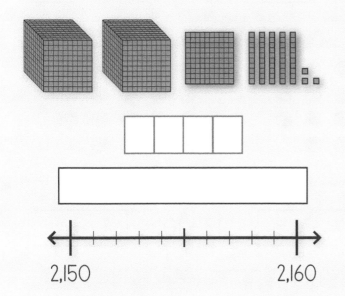

2,150   2,160

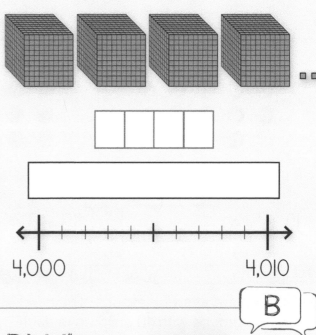

4,000   4,010

Number Riddles

2,247   4,247

4,052   2,053

2,253   3,227

4,012   2,152

3,267   2,154

4,000   3,999

Practice 👤

Complete.

Expanded Form	Number
5,000 + 900 + 60 + 2	5,962
3,000 + 400 + 50 + 7	
	6,831
	7,999
8,000 + 8	
4,000 + 40	

Complete.

$ _____

$ _____

Connect each number to its place on the number line.

2,993	2,999	3,004	3,006

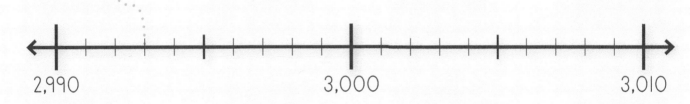

2,990   3,000   3,010

2,991	2,995	3,001	3,008

Match.

4,264 + 1		4,364
4,264 + 100		4,274
4,264 + 10		5,264
4,264 + 1,000		4,265

4,264 - 1		4,254
4,264 - 10		4,164
4,264 - 100		4,263
4,264 - 1,000		3,264

Review 👤 Match.

90 ÷ 10		5		30 ÷ 5
50 ÷ 10		6		40 ÷ 5
70 ÷ 10		7		45 ÷ 5
80 ÷ 10		8		25 ÷ 5
60 ÷ 10		9		35 ÷ 5

Complete.

$70 \times 3 = \boxed{}$

$40 \times 8 = \boxed{}$

$50 \times 5 = \boxed{}$

$90 \times 7 = \boxed{}$

$60 \times 8 = \boxed{}$

Complete with <, >, or =.

$\frac{4}{8} \bigcirc \frac{1}{8}$

$\frac{1}{6} \bigcirc \frac{1}{3}$

$\frac{3}{6} \bigcirc \frac{1}{2}$

Circle pairs that make 1,000.

450	550	125	875
650	250	850	225
350	750	150	775

Lesson Activities

| 3,678 | 5,070 | 4,000 | 6,999 |

$1,899 ◯ 2,015

$1,899

$2,015

4,600 ◯ 4,700

9,265 ◯ 9,256

8,791 ◯ 891

3,100 ◯ 3,040

| Greatest Possible Number | Least Possible Number |

11.2

Complete the circles with <, >, or =.

4,629 ◯ 5,000	3,890 ◯ 3,265	1,698 ◯ 698
7,001 ◯ 7,010	5,000 ◯ 4,000	6,245 ◯ 6,145
6,000 ◯ 5,999	4,309 ◯ 4,390	8,972 ◯ 8,972

Circle the greatest number in each group.

7,258	3,115	4,400
5,287	3,151	4,404
8,785	3,515	4,440
2,875	3,551	4,040
8,572	3,155	4,004

Write a number in the blank that makes the statement true.

5,000 > ☐   5,000 < ☐   5,000 = ☐

☐ < 3,946   ☐ > 3,946   ☐ = 3,946

Review

Color the problems that match the number in the star.

280

| 190 + 90 |
| 300 − 20 |
| 80 × 4 |

300

| 150 + 150 |
| 340 − 50 |
| 60 × 5 |

350

| 325 + 25 |
| 420 − 60 |
| 70 × 5 |

420

| 350 + 80 |
| 490 − 70 |
| 60 × 7 |

540

| 380 + 60 |
| 600 − 60 |
| 90 × 6 |

560

| 490 + 80 |
| 600 − 40 |
| 80 × 7 |

Round to the nearest hundred.

919	990	999	909	991	911

Solve. Write the equations you use.

Sofia earns $5 each time she shovels snow. How many times must she shovel snow to earn $30?

James earns $8 per hour for babysitting. If he babysits for 4 hours, how much does he earn?

Lesson Activities 👥

A

Multiplication Undercover (×7)

Player 1	7	14	21	28	35	42	49	56	63	70
Player 2	7	14	21	28	35	42	49	56	63	70

B

Distance Between Cities

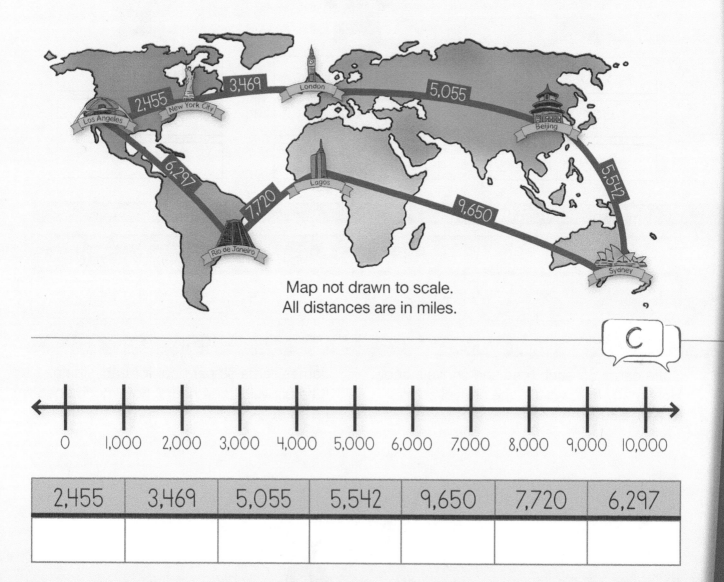

Map not drawn to scale.
All distances are in miles.

C

2,455	3,469	5,055	5,542	9,650	7,720	6,297

Practice 👤 Connect each number to its dot on the number line.

7,274	7,450	7,972

7,000   7,500   8,000

7,193	7,625	7,816

Round each number to the nearest thousand. Use the number line to help.

7,816	7,450	7,193	7,625	7,972	7,274

Round each number to the nearest thousand.

DICTIONARY
2,096
pages

About _____ pages

$4,999

About _____ dollars

1,894
Kilometers
→

About _____ kilometers

Review 👤 Complete.

3,000 + 4,000 = ☐

4,000 - 3,000 = ☐

300 + 400 = ☐

400 - 300 = ☐

Start ▶ 30 + 40 = ☐

40 - 30 = ☐

★ 5,120 + 1,650 = ☐

★ 3,750 - 1,520 = ☐

5,120 + 1,600 = ☐

3,750 - 1,500 = ☐

5,120 + 1,000 = ☐

3,750 - 1,000 = ☐

Complete.

18 ÷ 2 = ☐   40 ÷ 5 = ☐   16 ÷ 2 = ☐

25 ÷ 5 = ☐   12 ÷ 2 = ☐   20 ÷ 2 = ☐

45 ÷ 5 = ☐   14 ÷ 2 = ☐   30 ÷ 5 = ☐

Solve. Write the equations you use.

Jo has $4.38. She earns $3.75.
Then, she spends $2.49.
How much money does she have now?

$2.49

Lesson Activities

$2,600 +$ ☐ $= 3,000$

$8,900 +$ ☐ $= 9,000$

$6,500 +$ ☐ $= 7,000$

$4,300 +$ ☐ $= 5,000$

$1,200 +$ ☐ $= 2,000$

B

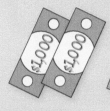 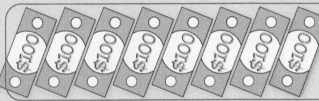 

$2,800 + 500 =$ ☐

$8,900 + 400 =$ ☐

$6,500 + 700 =$ ☐

$4,300 + 900 =$ ☐

$1,200 + 900 =$ ☐

C

Race to 10,000 Scoring Guide

 $= 100$

$= 200$

$= 300$

$= 400$

$= 500$

$= 600$

1 or 2 of a Kind $= 0$

4 of a Kind $= 900$

5 of a Kind $= 2,000$

6 of a Kind $= 3,000$

Practice 👤 Circle pairs that equal 5,000.

4,500	400	4,300	700
500	4,600	100	4,700
4,800	200	4,900	300

Complete.

Start → 3,700 + 300 = ☐
3,700 + 400 = ☐
3,700 + 500 = ☐

8,900 + 100 = ☐
8,900 + 400 = ☐
8,900 + 700 = ☐

6,500 + 500 = ☐
6,500 + 800 = ☐
6,500 + 900 = ☐

⭐ 7,750 + 250 = ☐
⭐ 7,750 + 450 = ☐
⭐ 7,750 + 950 = ☐

Solve. Write the equations you use.

Tim's mom tries to walk 8,000 steps per day. One day, she walks 7,400 steps. How many more steps does she need to walk to meet her goal?

Madison's family drives 800 miles to visit her grandparents. Then, they drive 800 miles home. How far do they drive in all?

Review ● Match.

20 ÷ 2	6	40 ÷ 5
14 ÷ 2	7	30 ÷ 5
18 ÷ 2	8	50 ÷ 5
16 ÷ 2	9	45 ÷ 5
12 ÷ 2	10	35 ÷ 5

Write the multiples in order.

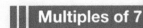

Multiples of 7 → | 7 | 14 | 21 | | | | | | | 70 |

Multiples of 8 → | 8 | 16 | | | | | | | | 80 |

Complete.

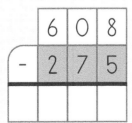

```
  4 5 7
+ 3 5 9
-------
```

```
  6 0 8
- 2 7 5
-------
```

Solve. Write the equations you use.

Josh organized his model cars. He has 4 shelves, and he put 6 cars on each shelf. He had 5 cars left, so he put them on his desk. How many model cars does Josh have?

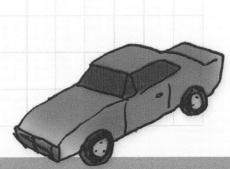

Lesson Activities

3,000 - 200 = ☐

4,000 - 600 = ☐

2,000 - 100 = ☐

5,000 - 400 = ☐

6,000 - 500 = ☐

8,000 - 900 = ☐

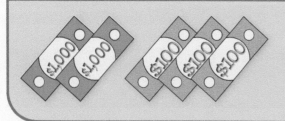

2,300 - 400 = ☐

3,100 - 200 = ☐

5,200 - 500 = ☐

2,600 - 800 = ☐

4,500 - 700 = ☐

Race to 0 Scoring Guide

  = 100

  = 200

  = 300

  = 400

  = 500

  = 600

1 or 2 of a Kind = 0

4 of a Kind = 900

5 of a Kind = 2,000

6 of a Kind = 3,000

Practice 👤 Match.

5,000 - 500	4,400	5,100 - 400
5,000 - 400	4,500	5,100 - 700
5,000 - 600	4,600	5,300 - 400
5,000 - 100	4,700	5,300 - 800
5,000 - 300	4,800	5,200 - 600
5,000 - 200	4,900	5,700 - 900

Complete.

7,000 →-500→ ☐ →-600→ ☐ →-400→ 5,500

8,000 →-900→ ☐ →-700→ ☐ →-400→ 6,000

9,000 →-800→ ☐ →-500→ ☐ →-700→ 7,000

⭐6,350 →-500→ ☐ →-900→ ☐ →-350→ 4,600

Review 👤 Write the multiples in order.

Multiples of 6 ➤	6	12	18							60

Multiples of 9 ➤	9	18								90

Find the perimeter and area.

6 ft.

5 ft.

Perimeter: _____

Area: _____

Write the time.

| : |

| : |

| : |

| : |

Solve. Write the equations you use.

Ava's family drove 274 miles in the morning and 189 miles in the afternoon. How far did they drive in all?

Ava's family drove 274 miles in the morning and 189 miles in the afternoon. How much farther did they drive in the morning than the afternoon?

Lesson Activities 👥

Estimate

	3,	9	8	4
+	2,	6	3	2

+ _____

Estimate

	4,	1	9	6
-	2,	8	7	9

- _____

Distance Between Cities

2,455
3,469
5,055
3,105
7,118
5,542
6,297
7,720
9,650

London
New York City
Los Angeles
Beijing
Lagos
Rio de Janeiro
Sydney

Map not drawn to scale.
All distances are in miles.

Itinerary	Total Distance Traveled	Difference in Flight Lengths
✈		
✈		
✈		
✈		

Practice   Complete.

	6,	9	2	7
+	1,	4	6	2

	4,	1	5	8
−	2,	6	4	1

	5,	0	6	5
−	3,	2	4	8

Use the ad to solve. Write the equations you use.

LARRY'S USED VEHICLES Big Sale!

Golf Cart $3,249

All-terrain Vehicle $4,950

Motorcycle $6,578

How much does it cost to buy the
golf cart and the all-terrain vehicle?

How much more does the motorcycle
cost than the golf cart?

You have $4,500. You buy the golf cart.
How much money do you have left?

How much does it cost to buy the
motorcycle and the golf cart?

Review 👤 Use the chart to complete the pictograph.

Favorite Season	Number of People
🌧 Winter	6
🌷 Spring	10
☀ Summer	14
🍂 Fall	8

Favorite season

Winter	😊 😊 😊
Spring	
Summer	
Fall	

😊 = 2 people

Complete.

$$\frac{2}{4} + \frac{1}{4} = \boxed{}$$

$$\frac{1}{3} + \frac{2}{3} = \boxed{}$$

$$\frac{3}{6} + \frac{2}{6} = \boxed{}$$

$$\frac{3}{4} - \frac{1}{4} = \boxed{}$$

$$\frac{3}{3} - \frac{1}{3} = \boxed{}$$

$$\frac{5}{6} - \frac{2}{6} = \boxed{}$$

Complete.

$$23 \div 5 = \boxed{}$$

$$23 \div 4 = \boxed{}$$

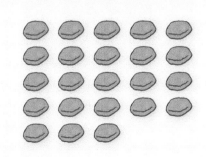

$$23 \div 10 = \boxed{}$$

Lesson Activities 👥

A

1,500
4,200
1,900

$1500

4200 Main Street

EST. 1900

B

Inventions Timeline

Telescope 1608

Telephone 1876

Television 1927

1600   1700   1800   1900   2000

Sewing Machine 1790

Steam Engine 1765

Airplane 1903

C

Practice 👤 Match.

two thousand four hundred		forty-five hundred
1,600		
three thousand seven hundred	2,400	sixteen hundred
four thousand five hundred	3,700	twenty-four hundred
one thousand six hundred	4,500	thirty-seven hundred

Write the current year in the chart. Then, use the chart to answer the questions.

Current year	
First person walks on the moon	1969
Pluto discovered	1930
Saturn's rings discovered	1610

How many years ago were Saturn's rings discovered?

How many years ago was Pluto discovered?

How many years ago did the first person walk on the moon?

11.7

Review 👤 Use the numbers to complete the blanks.
You will use each number once.

| 1 | 2 | 3 | 4 | 5 | 6 | 7 | 8 | 9 |

☐ × 3 = 6   3 × ☐ = 21   3 × ☐ = 9

☐ × 3 = 24   3 × ☐ = 3   3 × ☐ = 27

☐ × 3 = 12   3 × ☐ = 18   3 × ☐ = 15

Find the area and perimeter of each shape.

8 m
4 m

Perimeter: ☐
Area: ☐

6 in.
6 in.

Perimeter: ☐
Area: ☐

2 cm
10 cm

Perimeter: ☐
Area: ☐

Complete.

5 weeks, 2 days = ☐ days

4 weeks, 6 days = ☐ days

8 weeks, 3 days = ☐ days

⭐ 3 weeks, ☐ days = 24 days

Copy the shapes.

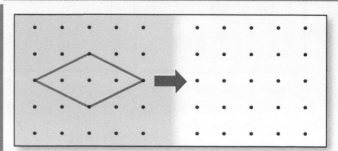

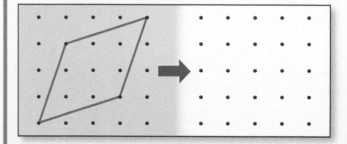

Unit Wrap-Up 👤 Write the value of each set of base-ten blocks.

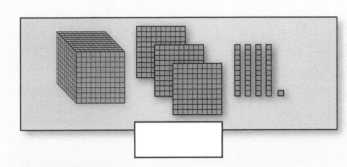

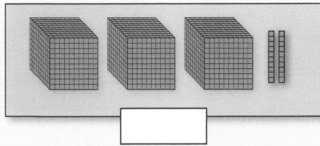

Connect each number to its place on the number line.

| 7,997 | 7,992 | 8,005 | 8,001 |

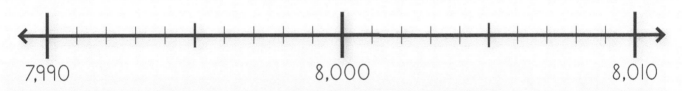

7,990   8,000   8,010

Round to the nearest thousand.

6,704	8,962	7,135	4,500

Complete.

Expanded Form	Number
5,000 + 400 + 20	
	6,125
9,000 + 9	
	4,078

Complete with <, >, or =.

3,768 ◯ 3,786

9,645 ◯ 9,642

4,000 ◯ 3,979

Unit Wrap-Up 👤 Match.

2,900 + 200	3,000	4,100 - 200	3,900
2,700 + 500	3,100	4,000 - 500	3,800
2,800 + 700	3,200	4,200 - 600	3,600
2,600 + 400	3,500	4,300 - 500	3,500

Complete the sequences.

Count by 1s: 7,307 ☐ ☐ ☐ ☐ 7,312

Count by 10s: 6,780 ☐ ☐ ☐ ☐ 6,830

Count by 100s: 4,700 ☐ ☐ ☐ ☐ 5,200

Complete.

```
   3,5 9 2
 +   4,4 4 6
 _____
```

```
   8,3 5 0
 -   3,6 2 8
 _____
```

Lesson Activities 👥

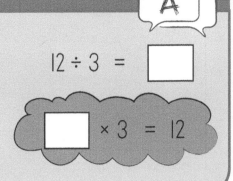

$12 \div 3 =$ ☐

☐ $\times 3 = 12$

$6 \div 3 =$ ☐ $9 \div 3 =$ ☐ $3 \div 3 =$ ☐

$15 \div 3 =$ ☐ $18 \div 3 =$ ☐ $30 \div 3 =$ ☐

$21 \div 3 =$ ☐ $27 \div 3 =$ ☐ $24 \div 3 =$ ☐

Climb and Slide

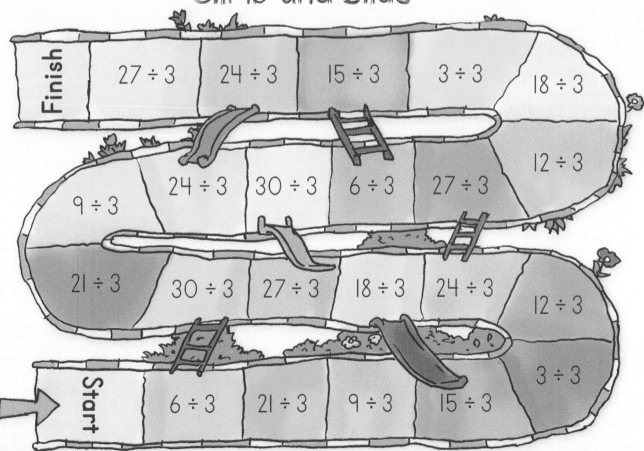

Practice 👤 Complete.

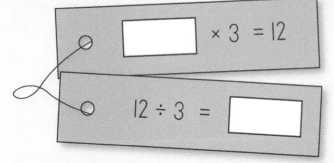

$\boxed{} \times 3 = 12$

$12 \div 3 = \boxed{}$

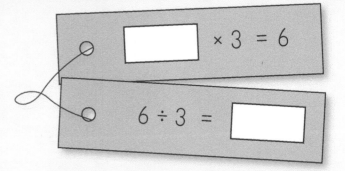

$\boxed{} \times 3 = 6$

$6 \div 3 = \boxed{}$

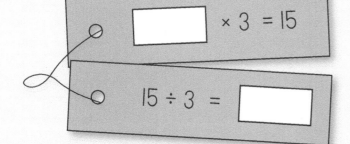

$\boxed{} \times 3 = 15$

$15 \div 3 = \boxed{}$

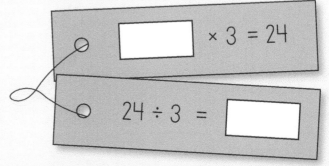

$\boxed{} \times 3 = 24$

$24 \div 3 = \boxed{}$

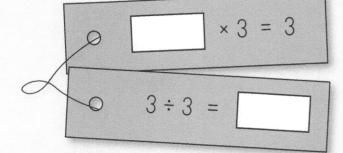

$\boxed{} \times 3 = 3$

$3 \div 3 = \boxed{}$

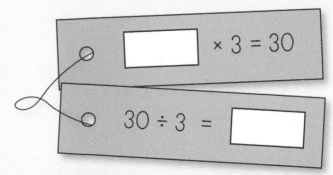

$\boxed{} \times 3 = 30$

$30 \div 3 = \boxed{}$

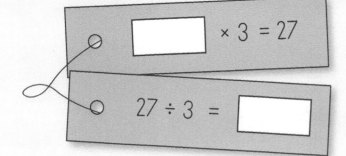

$\boxed{} \times 3 = 27$

$27 \div 3 = \boxed{}$

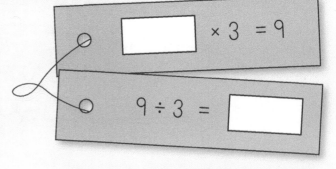

$\boxed{} \times 3 = 9$

$9 \div 3 = \boxed{}$

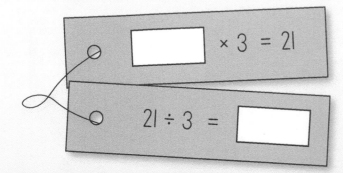

$\boxed{} \times 3 = 21$

$21 \div 3 = \boxed{}$

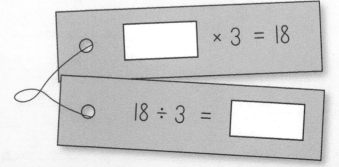

$\boxed{} \times 3 = 18$

$18 \div 3 = \boxed{}$

Review 👤 Draw a shape to match.

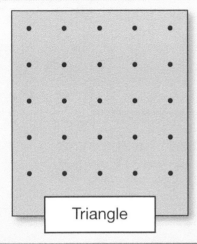

Triangle

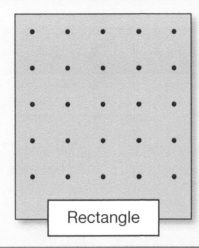

Rectangle

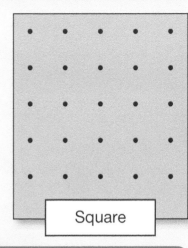

Square

Isabella made a bar graph to show how many people came to the skating rink each day. Use the bar graph to complete the chart and answer the questions.

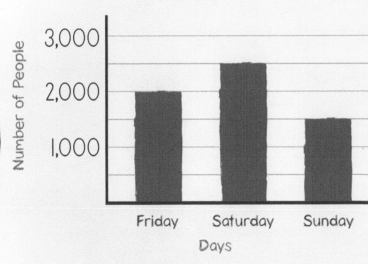

People at the Skating Rink

Day	Number of People
Friday	
Saturday	
Sunday	

How many more people came on Saturday than Friday?

How many fewer people came on Sunday than Saturday?

How many people came in all on Saturday and Sunday?

How many people came in all 3 days?

12.2

$$9 \div 2 = 4 \, R1$$

There is 1 brownie. 3 friends want to share it equally. How many brownies does each person get?

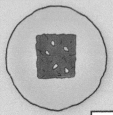

$1 \div 3 = \boxed{}$

There are 3 brownies. 1 friend wants to eat them all by himself! How many brownies does he get?

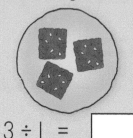

$3 \div 1 = \boxed{}$

$2 \div 1 = \boxed{}$ $4 \div 1 = \boxed{}$ $100 \div 1 = \boxed{}$

There are 0 brownies. 3 friends want to share them equally. How many brownies does each person get?

$0 \div 3 = \boxed{}$

There are 3 brownies. 0 friends want to share them equally. How many brownies does each person get?

$3 \div 0 = \boxed{}$

$0 \div 5 = \boxed{}$ $7 \div 0 = \boxed{}$ $0 \div 100 = \boxed{}$

$5 \div 0 = \boxed{}$ $0 \div 7 = \boxed{}$ $100 \div 0 = \boxed{}$

Practice

Complete the problems that can be solved.
Cross out the problems that cannot be solved.

$0 \div 3 =$ ☐ 0

$3 \div 0 =$ ☐

$6 \div 0 =$ ☐

$0 \div 6 =$ ☐

$8 \div 1 =$ ☐

$0 \div 8 =$ ☐

$0 \div 9 =$ ☐

$9 \div 0 =$ ☐

$1 \div 0 =$ ☐

$10 \div 1 =$ ☐

$0 \div 50 =$ ☐

$50 \div 0 =$ ☐

Complete.

$12 \div 3 =$ ☐

$9 \div 3 =$ ☐

$24 \div 3 =$ ☐

$30 \div 3 =$ ☐

$21 \div 3 =$ ☐

$15 \div 3 =$ ☐

$27 \div 3 =$ ☐

$18 \div 3 =$ ☐

$6 \div 3 =$ ☐

Solve. Write a division equation to match.

Amir buys 3 movie tickets. He pays $27.
How much does each movie ticket cost?

Brooklyn has 25 feet of ribbon.
She cuts it into pieces that are 5 feet long.
How many pieces does she get?

25 feet

☐ $\div$ ☐ $=$ ☐

☐ $\div$ ☐ $=$ ☐

Review 👤 Use the numbers to complete the blanks. You will use each number once.

| 1 | 2 | 3 | 4 | 5 | 6 | 7 | 8 | 9 |

☐ × 4 = 12	4 × ☐ = 20	4 × ☐ = 16
☐ × 4 = 32	4 × ☐ = 4	4 × ☐ = 36
☐ × 4 = 8	4 × ☐ = 28	4 × ☐ = 24

Complete with <, >, or =.

6×7 ◯ 40

7×7 ◯ 50

8×6 ◯ 50

9×6 ◯ 50

9×9 ◯ 80

Round to the nearest thousand.

6,742	
8,499	
3,500	
2,077	
4,601	

Complete the sequences.

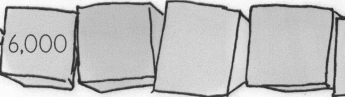

Count by 5s — 6,000 ... 6,025

Count by 10s — 5,480 ... 5,530

Lesson Activities

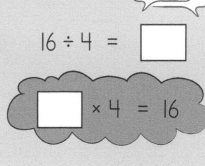

A

16 ÷ 4 = ☐

☐ × 4 = 16

12 ÷ 4 = ☐   20 ÷ 4 = ☐   32 ÷ 4 = ☐

24 ÷ 4 = ☐   8 ÷ 4 = ☐   4 ÷ 4 = ☐

28 ÷ 4 = ☐   40 ÷ 4 = ☐   36 ÷ 4 = ☐

B

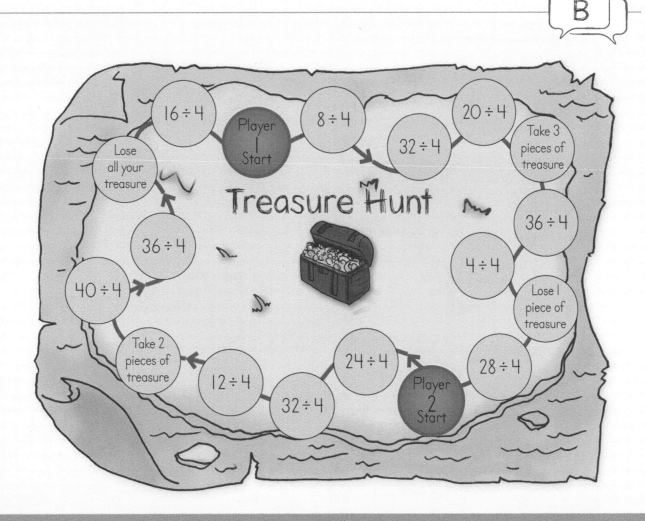

Treasure Hunt

12.3

Practice Complete.

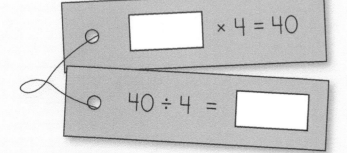

$\boxed{} \times 4 = 8$

$8 \div 4 = \boxed{}$

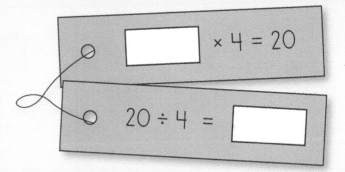

$\boxed{} \times 4 = 20$

$20 \div 4 = \boxed{}$

$\boxed{} \times 4 = 40$

$40 \div 4 = \boxed{}$

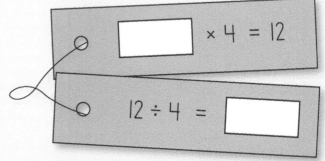

$\boxed{} \times 4 = 12$

$12 \div 4 = \boxed{}$

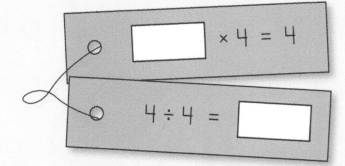

$\boxed{} \times 4 = 4$

$4 \div 4 = \boxed{}$

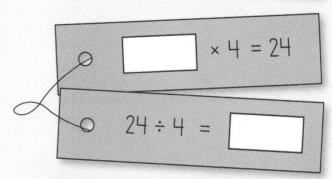

$\boxed{} \times 4 = 24$

$24 \div 4 = \boxed{}$

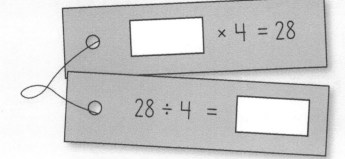

$\boxed{} \times 4 = 28$

$28 \div 4 = \boxed{}$

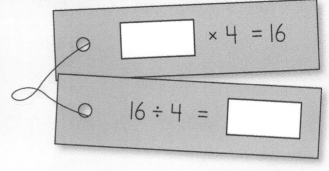

$\boxed{} \times 4 = 16$

$16 \div 4 = \boxed{}$

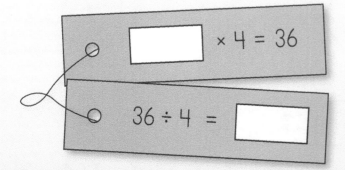

$\boxed{} \times 4 = 36$

$36 \div 4 = \boxed{}$

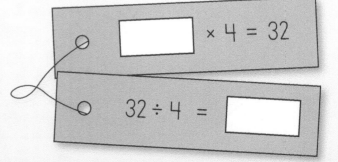

$\boxed{} \times 4 = 32$

$32 \div 4 = \boxed{}$

Review · Circle the more sensible unit for each item.

Area of a sticky note

| 4 sq. ft. | 4 sq. in. |

Area of a mirror

| 3 sq. ft. | 3 sq. in. |

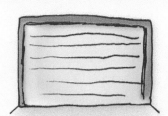

Area of a garage door

| 15 sq. yd. | 15 sq. ft. |

Color the multiples in order from Start to End.

Multiples of 8

16	24	32	40	44
8	20	36	48	54
14	28	40	56	64
18	36	44	63	72
12	21	35	70	80

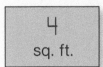 Start

END

Complete.

3,500 + 500 =

4,900 + 400 =

6,000 - 200 =

7,100 - 300 =

Solve. Write the equations you use.

A sandwich costs $6.39.
A drink costs $4.48 less
than a sandwich.
How much does it cost to
buy a sandwich and a drink?

Lesson 12.3

93

12.4

Lesson Activities 👥

12 children split into 2 groups.
How many children are in each group?

$$12 \div 2 = \boxed{}$$

↑ total ↑ number of groups ↑ size of each group

12 children split into groups of 2.
How many groups do they make?

$$12 \div 2 = \boxed{}$$

↑ total ↑ size of each group ↑ number of groups

There are 30 children at gymnastics lessons. The coaches divide the children into 5 equal groups. How many children are in each group?

20 children carpool together to the museum. 4 children fit in each car. How many cars do they need?

Eden arranges 24 chairs for the piano recital. She makes 3 rows. How many chairs are in each row?

Simon has 12 inches of yarn.
He cuts the yarn into 4 equal pieces.
How long is each piece?

Practice   👤   **Complete.**

40 ÷ 4 = ☐   24 ÷ 4 = ☐   16 ÷ 4 = ☐

8 ÷ 4 = ☐   20 ÷ 4 = ☐   32 ÷ 4 = ☐

28 ÷ 4 = ☐   36 ÷ 4 = ☐   12 ÷ 4 = ☐

27 ÷ 3 = ☐   21 ÷ 3 = ☐   24 ÷ 3 = ☐

6 ÷ 1 = ☐   12 ÷ 1 = ☐   20 ÷ 1 = ☐

Solve. Write the equations you use.

4 donuts fit in a box.
If you have 24 donuts, how many boxes can you fill completely?

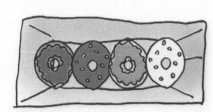

There are 15 children on the soccer team.
They split into 5 equal groups at practice.
How many children are in each group?

Sara has 28 feet of rope. She cuts the rope into pieces that are 4 feet long. How many pieces does she get?

4 friends earn $20 at a lemonade stand.
They share the money equally.
How much money does each person get?

Review

Use the numbers to complete the blanks.
You will use each number once.

| 1 | 2 | 3 | 4 | 5 | 6 | 7 | 8 | 9 |

$\boxed{} \times 6 = 24$ $6 \times \boxed{} = 36$ $6 \times \boxed{} = 18$

$\boxed{} \times 6 = 30$ $6 \times \boxed{} = 12$ $6 \times \boxed{} = 48$

$\boxed{} \times 6 = 54$ $6 \times \boxed{} = 6$ $6 \times \boxed{} = 42$

Complete with <, >, or =.

$6 \times 6 \bigcirc 35$

$6 \times 7 \bigcirc 40$

$8 \times 7 \bigcirc 60$

$8 \times 8 \bigcirc 60$

$8 \times 9 \bigcirc 70$

Complete.

$65 - 63 = \boxed{}$

$71 - 65 = \boxed{}$

$127 - 125 = \boxed{}$

$153 - 148 = \boxed{}$

Complete the sequences.

Count by 2s

5,100   5,110

Count by 20s

5,100   5,200

Lesson Activities

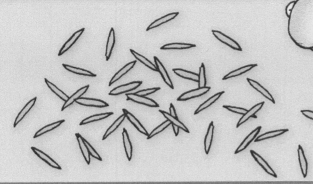

$42 \div 6 = \boxed{}$

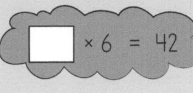

$\boxed{} \times 6 = 42$

$60 \div 6 = \boxed{}$ $12 \div 6 = \boxed{}$ $24 \div 6 = \boxed{}$

$30 \div 6 = \boxed{}$ $6 \div 6 = \boxed{}$ $36 \div 6 = \boxed{}$

$54 \div 6 = \boxed{}$ $48 \div 6 = \boxed{}$ $18 \div 6 = \boxed{}$

B

Dice Tic-Tac-Toe

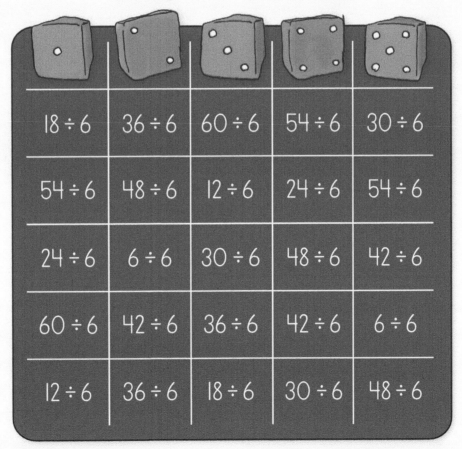

$18 \div 6$	$36 \div 6$	$60 \div 6$	$54 \div 6$	$30 \div 6$
$54 \div 6$	$48 \div 6$	$12 \div 6$	$24 \div 6$	$54 \div 6$
$24 \div 6$	$6 \div 6$	$30 \div 6$	$48 \div 6$	$42 \div 6$
$60 \div 6$	$42 \div 6$	$36 \div 6$	$42 \div 6$	$6 \div 6$
$12 \div 6$	$36 \div 6$	$18 \div 6$	$30 \div 6$	$48 \div 6$

Practice 👤 Complete.

☐ × 6 = 18

18 ÷ 6 = ☐

☐ × 6 = 30

30 ÷ 6 = ☐

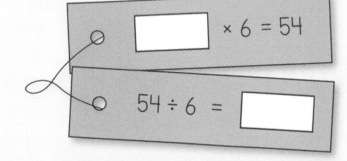 ☐ × 6 = 54

54 ÷ 6 = ☐

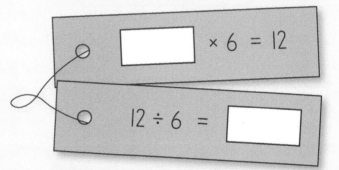 ☐ × 6 = 12

12 ÷ 6 = ☐

☐ × 6 = 24

24 ÷ 6 = ☐

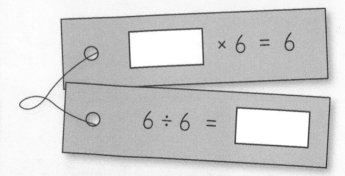 ☐ × 6 = 6

6 ÷ 6 = ☐

☐ × 6 = 60

60 ÷ 6 = ☐

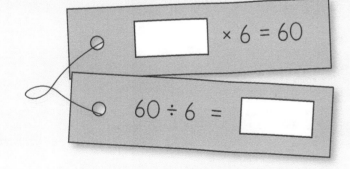 ☐ × 6 = 42

42 ÷ 6 = ☐

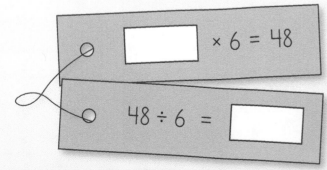 ☐ × 6 = 48

48 ÷ 6 = ☐

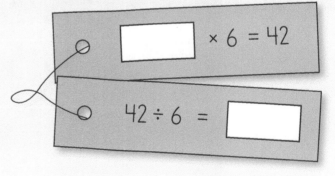 ☐ × 6 = 36

36 ÷ 6 = ☐

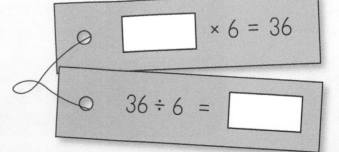

Review 👤 Complete the equivalent fractions.

$$\frac{1}{2} = \frac{}{4}$$

$$\frac{1}{2} = \frac{}{6}$$

$$\frac{1}{2} = \frac{}{8}$$

Color the multiples in order from Start to End.

Multiples of 7

Start →

7	14	21	28	35
12	16	54	49	42
24	48	64	56	60
45	36	40	63	70
35	30	32	72	80

END

Complete.

	3,	5	0	8
+	2,	7	6	4

Solve.

You pay the clerk $10.00.
How much change do you get?

$7.85

Change
$ _____

Copy the lines.

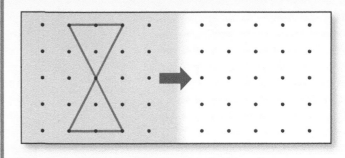

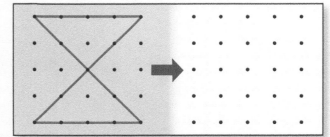

Lesson Activities 👥

A

20 Striped Chocolates
(4 in each box)

$20 \div 4 = \boxed{}$ $4\overline{)20}$

15 Caramel Chocolates
(5 in each box)

14 Cherry Chocolates
(7 in each box)

24 Dark Chocolates
(6 in each box)

B

Dice Tic-Tac-Toe

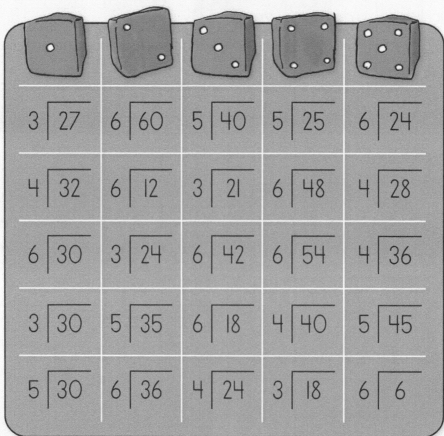

$3\overline{)27}$	$6\overline{)60}$	$5\overline{)40}$	$5\overline{)25}$	$6\overline{)24}$
$4\overline{)32}$	$6\overline{)12}$	$3\overline{)21}$	$6\overline{)48}$	$4\overline{)28}$
$6\overline{)30}$	$3\overline{)24}$	$6\overline{)42}$	$6\overline{)54}$	$4\overline{)36}$
$3\overline{)30}$	$5\overline{)35}$	$6\overline{)18}$	$4\overline{)40}$	$5\overline{)45}$
$5\overline{)30}$	$6\overline{)36}$	$4\overline{)24}$	$3\overline{)18}$	$6\overline{)6}$

Practice 👤 Complete.

$3\overline{)15}$ $4\overline{)24}$ $5\overline{)35}$ $4\overline{)40}$ $2\overline{)16}$

$2\overline{)10}$ $3\overline{)27}$ $4\overline{)36}$ $5\overline{)40}$ $4\overline{)32}$

$6\overline{)12}$ $6\overline{)60}$ $6\overline{)24}$ $6\overline{)18}$ $6\overline{)36}$

$6\overline{)6}$ $6\overline{)30}$ $6\overline{)48}$ $6\overline{)42}$ $6\overline{)54}$

Solve. Write each problem with a division bracket.

You need 35 pencils.
How many packs should you buy?

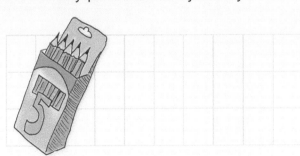

You need 10 staplers.
How many packs should you buy?

You need 90 markers.
How many packs should you buy?

You need 18 scissors.
How many packs should you buy?

12.6

Review   Complete.

9,	7	6	8
- 4,	2	8	5

3,	0	9	7
- 1,	6	4	4

6,	0	0	0
- 3,	8	5	0

Complete the equivalent fractions.

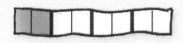

$\frac{1}{4} = \frac{}{8}$

$\frac{2}{4} = \frac{}{8}$

$\frac{3}{4} = \frac{}{8}$

$\frac{1}{3} = \frac{}{6}$

$\frac{2}{3} = \frac{}{6}$

$\frac{3}{3} = \frac{}{6}$

Use the grid lines to find the area of each shape. Circle the correct units.

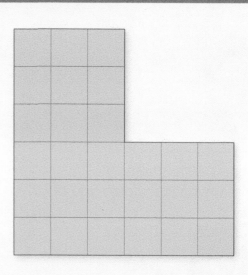

□ sq. in.
sq. cm

□ sq. in.
sq. cm

Lesson Activities 👥

Hit the Target

| 41 | 37 | 65 | 50 | 46 |

The CHOCOLATE SHOP

Striped Chocolates

4 | 2 | 3

full boxes

chocolates in the full boxes

chocolates left

Caramel Chocolates

5 | 1 | 6

full boxes

chocolates in the full boxes

chocolates left

Cherry Chocolates

3 | 2 | 0

full boxes

chocolates in the full boxes

chocolates left

Dark Chocolates

2 | 1 | 9

full boxes

chocolates in the full boxes

chocolates left

Milk Chocolates

1 | 0 | 4 | 3

full boxes

chocolates in the full boxes

chocolates left

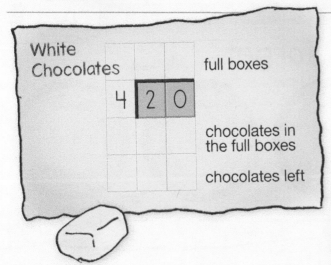

White Chocolates

4 2 0

full boxes

chocolates in the full boxes

chocolates left

Almond Chocolates

6 3 1

full boxes

chocolates in the full boxes

chocolates left

Practice

Color the problems that match the number in the star.

5

| 15 ÷ 3 |
| 24 ÷ 4 |
| 30 ÷ 6 |

8

| 24 ÷ 3 |
| 32 ÷ 4 |
| 42 ÷ 6 |

4

| 18 ÷ 3 |
| 16 ÷ 4 |
| 24 ÷ 6 |

6

| 18 ÷ 3 |
| 24 ÷ 4 |
| 48 ÷ 6 |

9

| 30 ÷ 3 |
| 36 ÷ 4 |
| 54 ÷ 6 |

7

| 21 ÷ 3 |
| 32 ÷ 4 |
| 42 ÷ 6 |

Review

Write the time.

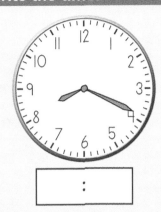

| : | | : | | : | | : |

Color the multiples in order from Start to End.

Multiples of 9

24	30	32	35	80
18	27	36	40	90	**END**
9	12	45	48	81
15	20	54	63	72
21	25	56	70	64

Start → 9

Complete.

$60 \times 4 =$ ☐

$70 \times 9 =$ ☐

$70 \times 6 =$ ☐

$40 \times 5 =$ ☐

$80 \times 8 =$ ☐

Complete.

Expanded Form	Number
$2,000 + 900 + 80 + 4$	
	6,245
$3,000 + 8$	
	9,040
	3,107

Solve.

Aaron finds $\frac{7}{8}$ of a leftover pizza in the fridge. He eats $\frac{1}{8}$ of the pizza.

What fraction of the whole pizza is left?

12.8

Lesson Activities 👥

Long Division

1. Divide — How many groups can I make?

2. Multiply — How many are in the groups?

3. Subtract — How many are left?

3 ⌐2 2

1. Divide

2. Multiply

3. Subtract

2 ⌐1 7   5 ⌐2 7   3 ⌐2 0   4 ⌐3 1

Roll and Divide

Player 1	1 9	2 3	2 8	Sum of remainders
Player 2	1 9	2 3	2 8	Sum of remainders

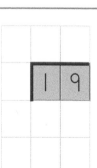

Practice 👤 Complete. Follow the steps.

1. Divide
2. Multiply
3. Subtract

2 | 1 | 1   5 | 2 | 4   3 | 1 | 7   4 | 1 | 3

Complete.

24 ÷ 3 = ☐

27 ÷ 3 = ☐

Start 30 ÷ 3 = ☐

28 ÷ 4 = ☐

24 ÷ 4 = ☐

20 ÷ 4 = ☐

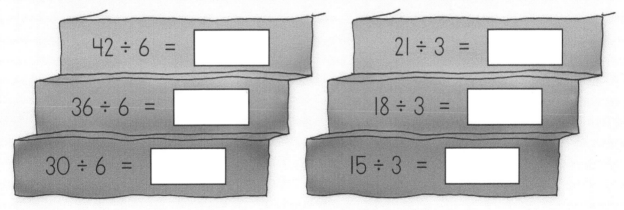

42 ÷ 6 = ☐

36 ÷ 6 = ☐

30 ÷ 6 = ☐

21 ÷ 3 = ☐

18 ÷ 3 = ☐

15 ÷ 3 = ☐

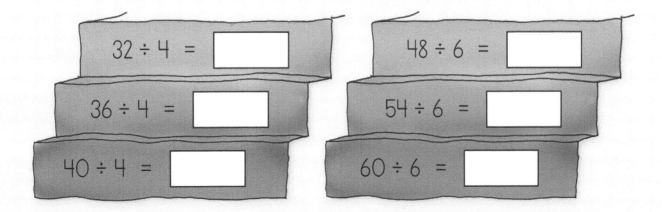

32 ÷ 4 = ☐

36 ÷ 4 = ☐

40 ÷ 4 = ☐

48 ÷ 6 = ☐

54 ÷ 6 = ☐

60 ÷ 6 = ☐

Review 👤 Find the perimeter and area of each rectangle.

8 m

6 m

Perimeter: ☐

Area: ☐

9 m

9 m

Perimeter: ☐

Area: ☐

Label the numbers on the number line.

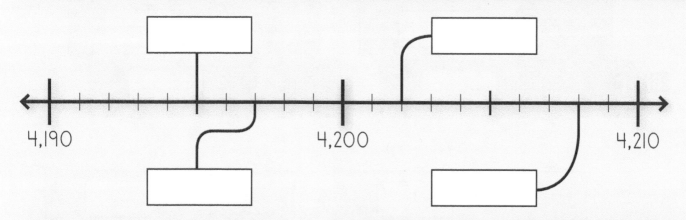

4,190   4,200   4,210

Complete with <, >, or =.

$\dfrac{5}{8}$ ◯ $\dfrac{3}{8}$

$\dfrac{1}{4}$ ◯ $\dfrac{1}{2}$

2 ◯ $\dfrac{1}{2}$

★ $3\dfrac{1}{4}$ ◯ $2\dfrac{3}{4}$

★ $\dfrac{7}{3}$ ◯ $\dfrac{8}{3}$

Match.

9 × 8		56
8 × 8		63
9 × 7		64
9 × 9		72
8 × 7		81

Lesson Activities

1. Divide
2. Multiply
3. Subtract

4 | 2 3   5 | 3 2   3 | 2 5   6 | 2 0

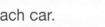

There are 32 children at gymnastics lessons.
The teachers divide the children into
5 groups.
They make the groups as even as possible.
How many children are in each group?

23 children carpool together
to the museum.
4 children fit in each car.
How many cars do they need?

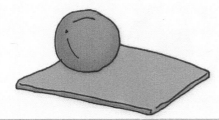

Eden arranges 25 chairs for the piano recital.
She makes 3 rows.
Then, she puts away any extra chairs.
How many chairs are in each row?

Simon has 20 inches of yarn.
He cuts the yarn into as many
6-inch-long pieces as he can.
How much yarn is left over?

12.9

Practice

Complete. Follow the steps.

1. Divide
2. Multiply
3. Subtract

4 | 2 5   5 | 1 7   4 | 3 1   4 | 2 1

**Solve. Use the completed problems above to help find the answers.
You do not need to write equations for the problems.**

4 donuts fit in a box.
If you have 25 donuts, how many boxes
can you fill completely?

There are 17 children on the soccer team.
They split into 5 groups.
They make the groups as equal as possible.
How many children are in each group?

Sara has 31 feet of rope. She cuts the rope
into pieces that are 4 feet long.
How much rope is left over?

⭐ 4 friends earn $21 at a lemonade
stand. They share the money equally.
How much money does each
person get?

Review

Split the rectangle into smaller rectangles.
Then, find the area of the whole rectangle.

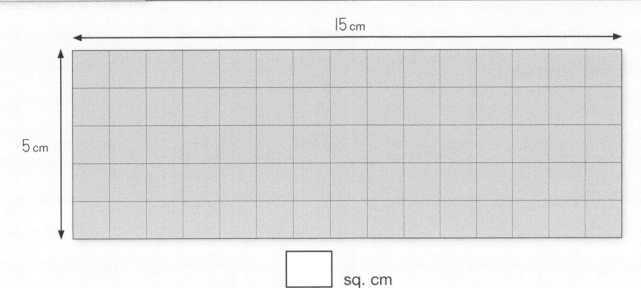

15 cm

5 cm

☐ sq. cm

Complete.	Circle the least number in each row.

$$\frac{5}{8} + \frac{2}{8} = \boxed{}$$

3,294   3,094   3,904

$$\frac{1}{6} + \frac{4}{6} = \boxed{}$$

5,065   5,056   5,650

$$\frac{3}{3} - \frac{1}{3} = \boxed{}$$

8,011   8,101   8,010

★ $$\frac{5}{3} - \frac{1}{3} = \boxed{}$$

Solve.

40 ÷ 10 = ☐   20 ÷ 4 = ☐   24 ÷ 6 = ☐

40 ÷ 5 = ☐   20 ÷ 2 = ☐   24 ÷ 3 = ☐

28 ÷ 4 = ☐   36 ÷ 6 = ☐   70 ÷ 10 = ☐

28 ÷ 2 = ☐   ★ 36 ÷ 3 = ☐   ★ 70 ÷ 5 = ☐

Unit Wrap-Up 👤 Complete.

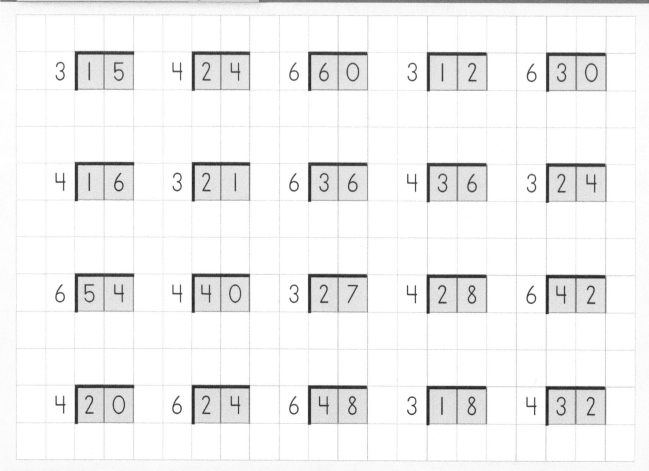

Complete. Cross out any problems that cannot be solved.

$0 \div 4 =$ ☐ $6 \div 0 =$ ☐ $0 \div 127 =$ ☐

$4 \div 0 =$ ☐ $0 \div 6 =$ ☐ $127 \div 0 =$ ☐

Match each number in the equation to the correct word.

$$16 \div 5 = 3 \text{ R}1$$

| divisor | remainder | dividend | quotient |

Unit Wrap-Up

Complete. Follow the steps.

1. Divide
2. Multiply
3. Subtract

$$5 \boxed{2\ 4} \qquad 3 \boxed{2\ 5} \qquad 6 \boxed{1\ 9} \qquad 4 \boxed{3\ 9}$$

Solve. Write the equations you use.

Darius has 26 googly eyes. He puts 4 googly eyes on each monster puppet. He makes as many puppets as he can. How many googly eyes does he have left over?

There are 27 children at swim lessons. They split into 3 groups and make the groups as equal as possible. How many children are in each group?

Mariana helps her grandpa plant peas. They have 24 seeds. They plant 6 seeds in each row. How many rows do they plant?

Brayden helps his mom decorate for a party. They blow up 50 balloons and tie them in 6 bunches. They make the bunches as equal as possible. How many balloons are in each bunch?

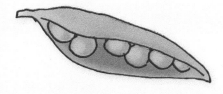

Lesson Activities 👥

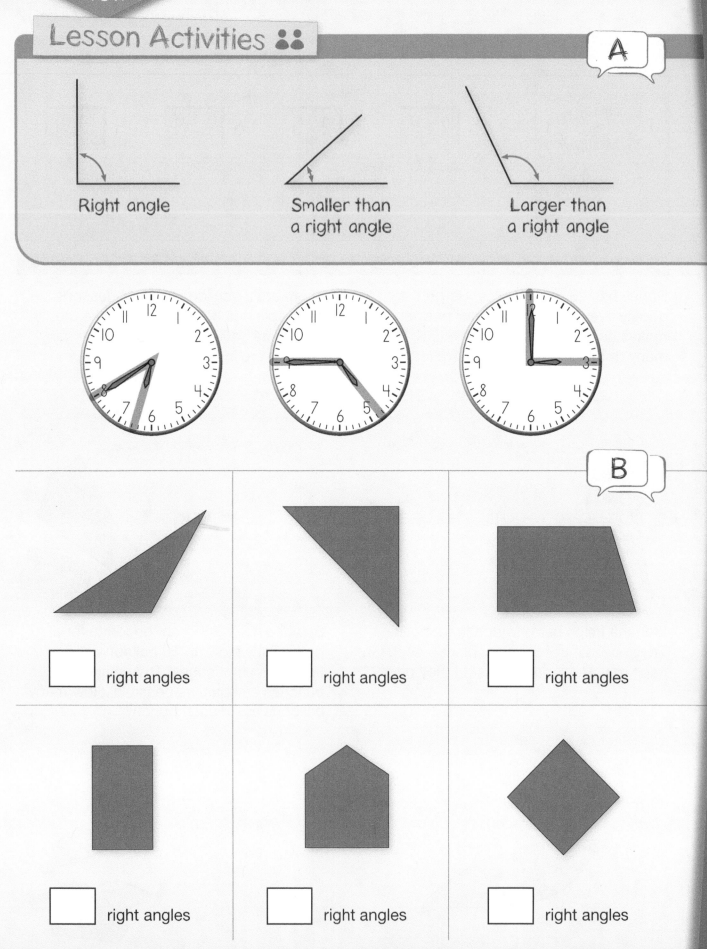

Right angle

Smaller than
a right angle

Larger than
a right angle

B

☐ right angles

☐ right angles

☐ right angles

☐ right angles

☐ right angles

☐ right angles

Practice 👤 Circle the description that matches the highlighted angle.

Right angle
Smaller than a right angle
Larger than a right angle

Right angle
Smaller than a right angle
Larger than a right angle

Right angle
Smaller than a right angle
Larger than a right angle

Right angle
Smaller than a right angle
Larger than a right angle

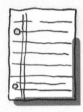

Right angle
Smaller than a right angle
Larger than a right angle

Right angle
Smaller than a right angle
Larger than a right angle

Tell how many right angles each shape has.

☐ right angles

☐ right angles

☐ right angles

☐ right angles

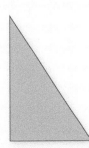

☐ right angles

☐ right angles

Review   Complete. Follow the steps.

1. Divide
2. Multiply
3. Subtract

```
2 | 1 | 7      5 | 4 | 2      4 | 3 | 7      3 | 2 | 8
```

Write the numbers that come before and after each number.

Before		After
3,464	3,465	3,466
	8,949	
	6,100	
	7,000	
	4,003	

Complete.

1 year = ☐ months

1 week = ☐ days

1 day = ☐ hours

1 hour = ☐ minutes

1 minute = ☐ seconds

Complete.

36 ÷ 4 = ☐   24 ÷ 4 = ☐   40 ÷ 4 = ☐

42 ÷ 6 = ☐   40 ÷ 5 = ☐   24 ÷ 3 = ☐

60 ÷ 6 = ☐   36 ÷ 6 = ☐   18 ÷ 2 = ☐

18 ÷ 3 = ☐   32 ÷ 4 = ☐   30 ÷ 3 = ☐

Lesson Activities

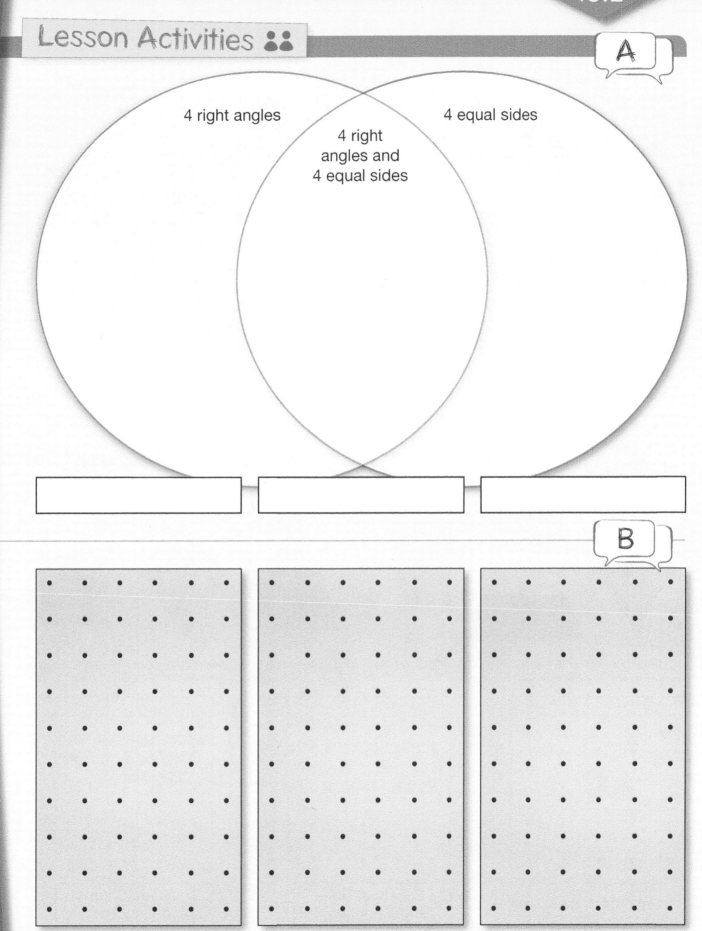

4 right angles

4 right angles and 4 equal sides

4 equal sides

Practice

Follow the directions for each group of shapes.

Circle the squares.
X the shapes that are not squares.

Circle the quadrilaterals.
X the shapes that are not quadrilaterals.

Circle the rectangles.
X the shapes that are not rectangles.

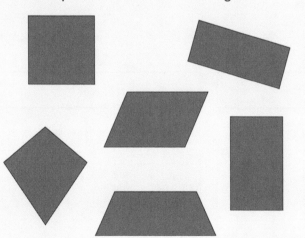

Circle the rhombuses.
X the shapes that are not rhombuses.

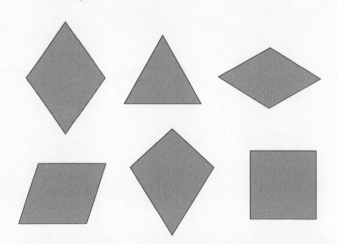

Draw a quadrilateral that matches each description.

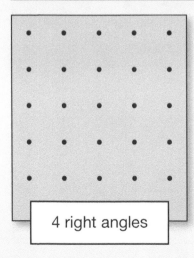

4 right angles

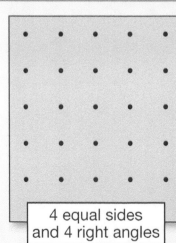

4 equal sides
and 4 right angles

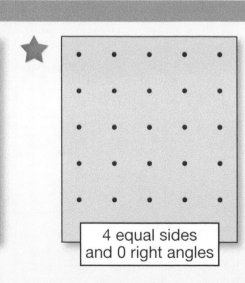

4 equal sides
and 0 right angles

Review

Write the time.

  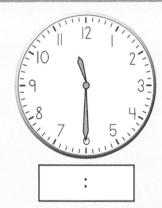 

| : | | : | | : | | : |

Complete.

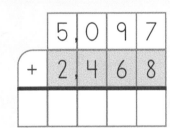

```
  5 , 0 9 7
+ 2 , 4 6 8
```

```
  5 , 0 9 7
- 2 , 4 6 8
```

Complete.

6	3 0		3	3 0		4	3 6
6	4 2		6	5 4		3	2 7
4	2 8		5	4 5		6	4 8

Solve. Write the equations you use to solve the problems.

There are 36 children at baseball practice.
They divide into 4 groups.
How many children are in each group?

There are 39 children at baseball practice.
They divide into 4 groups.
How many children are in each group?

Lesson Activities 👥

Pentomino Rules

- Every pentomino has 5 squares.

- Each square must touch at least one other square.

- Squares may only touch along their edges. They must touch from corner to corner.

Pentominoes

Not Pentominoes

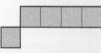

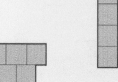

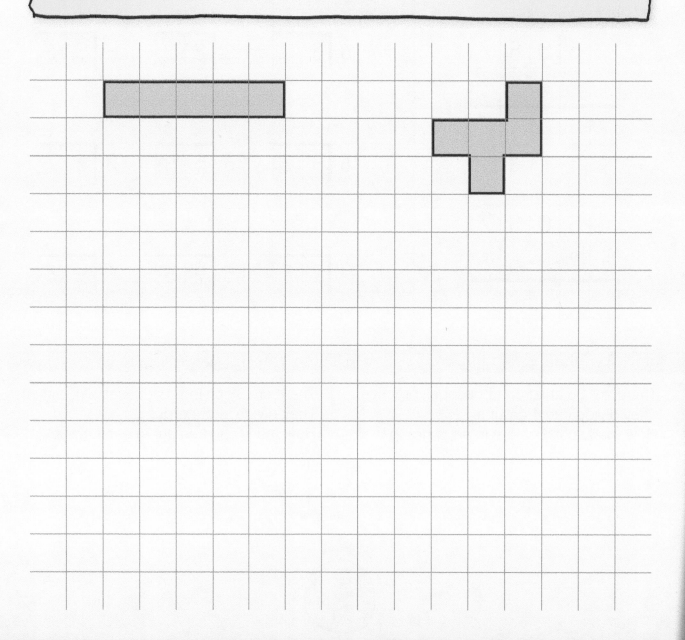

Practice

Find two different ways to cover each shape with pentominoes. Draw lines to show where you put each piece.

Review   Complete. Follow the steps.

| 1. Divide |
| 2. Multiply |
| 3. Subtract |

5 | 2 | 9   4 | 2 | 9   3 | 2 | 9   6 | 2 | 9

Round to the nearest dollar.

$9.99	$5.55	$7.77	$3.33	$4.44	$1.11

Color the circles to match.

$2 \frac{1}{4}$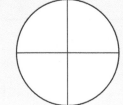

$1 \frac{5}{6}$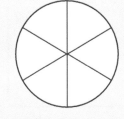

$\frac{7}{8}$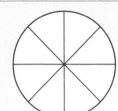

$2 \frac{1}{2}$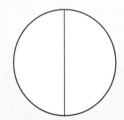

Complete with <, >, or =.

6 × 6 ◯ 35

8 × 7 ◯ 50

8 × 6 ◯ 50

7 × 7 ◯ 50

9 × 7 ◯ 60

9 × 9 ◯ 80

6 × 7 ◯ 40

8 × 8 ◯ 60

Lesson Activities 👥

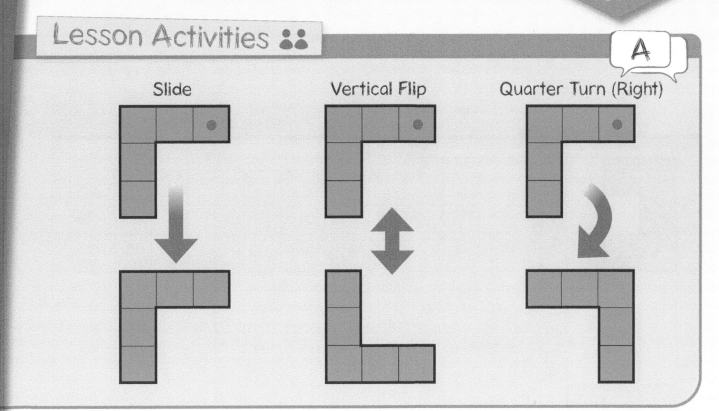

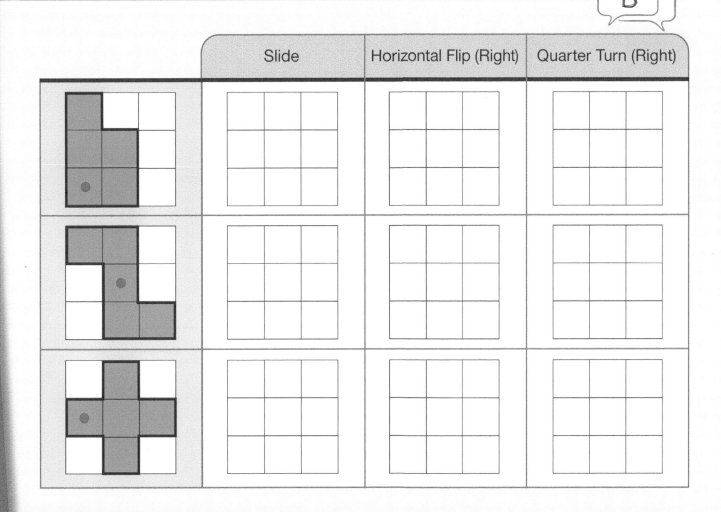

Practice 👤

Draw how each pentomino looks after a slide, horizontal flip to the right, and quarter turn to the right.

	Slide	Horizontal Flip (Right)	Quarter Turn (Right)

Review

Write the time.

| : | | : | | : | | : |

Complete.

÷ 3	
18	
27	
24	
21	
30	

÷ 4	
40	
28	
32	
36	
24	

÷ 6	
60	
36	
48	
42	
54	

Complete.

2 more than 2,658 is ___

20 more than 2,658 is ___

200 more than 2,658 is ___

2,000 more than 2,658 is ___

2 less than 2,658 is ___

20 less than 2,658 is ___

200 less than 2,658 is ___

2,000 less than 2,658 is ___

Solve.

You pay the clerk $6.00.
How much change do you get?

Change
$ ___

You pay the clerk $10.00.
How much change do you get?

Change
$ ___

Lesson Activities 👥

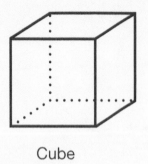

Cube

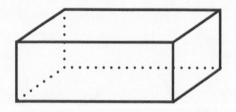

Rectangular prism

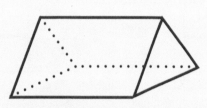

Triangular prism

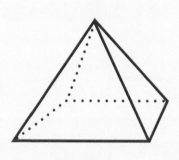

Pyramid

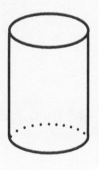

Cylinder

Cone

B

	Faces	Edges	Vertices
Cube			
Rectangular prism			
Triangular prism			
Pyramid			

Practice 👤 Match each shape to its name.

  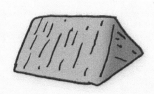  

| Triangular prism | Cone | Cylinder | Rectangular prism | Cube |

Find three things in your home that have each shape. Write their names.

Solid Shape Scavenger Hunt

Cube	Rectangular prism
Cone	Cylinder

Copy the shapes.

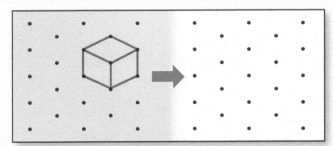 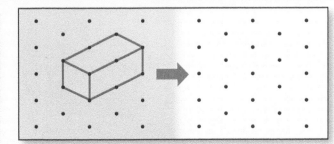

13.5

Review 👤 Circle pairs that make 60.

55	35	36	24
5	25	34	46
15	45	26	14

Complete the sequences.

Count by **25s** 4,550 ___ ___ ___ ___ 4,675

Count by **50s** 4,550 ___ ___ ___ ___ 4,800

Complete.

$8 \times 9 =$ ☐ $6 \times 8 =$ ☐ $9 \times 9 =$ ☐

$7 \times 7 =$ ☐ $9 \times 7 =$ ☐ $7 \times 8 =$ ☐

$6 \times 9 =$ ☐ $8 \times 8 =$ ☐ $6 \times 7 =$ ☐

Solve. Write the equations you use.

Daniel has $8.00. He spends $1.25 on gum and $5.75 on trading cards. How much money does he have left?

Unit Wrap-Up

Circle the description that matches the highlighted angle.

Right angle
Smaller than a right angle
Larger than a right angle

Right angle
Smaller than a right angle
Larger than a right angle

Right angle
Smaller than a right angle
Larger than a right angle

Tell how many right angles each shape has.

[ ] right angles

[ ] right angles

[ ] right angles

Write the word that describes all the shapes in each group.

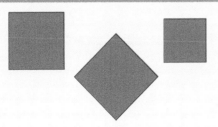

[   ]

[   ]

rhombuses

•

rectangles

•

quadrilaterals

•

squares

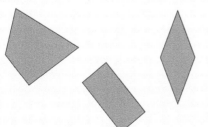

[   ]

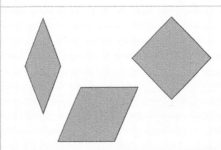

[   ]

Unit Wrap-Up

Use the words in the word bank to label the shapes.

cube	○ rectangular prism	○ cylinder
cone	○ triangular prism	○ pyramid

 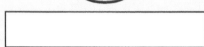 

 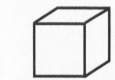 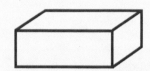

Complete the chart to match each shape.

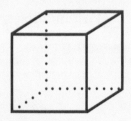 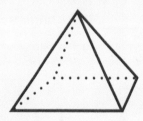 

Faces	
Edges	
Vertices	

Faces	
Edges	
Vertices	

Faces	
Edges	
Vertices	

Cover the shape with pentominoes. Draw lines to show where you put each piece.

 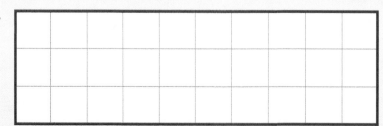

Lesson Activities

Science Museum Schedule

Tornado Vortex every 5 min.	Morning	9:25			
	Afternoon				3:05
Lightning every 10 min.	Morning	10:40			
	Afternoon				2:20
Chemistry Fun every 30 min.	Morning	9:20			
	Afternoon				1:30
Reptile Talk every 15 min.	Morning	10:45			
	Afternoon				4:30

Practice 👤 Write the time.

:   :   :   :

:   :   :   :

Complete the sequences.

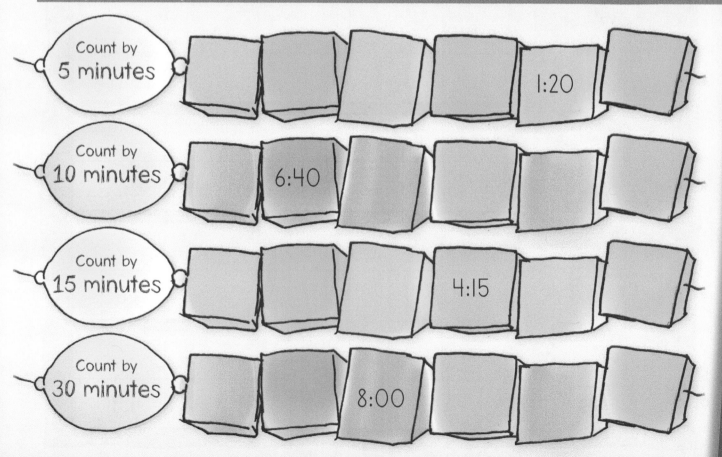

Count by 5 minutes   1:20

Count by 10 minutes   6:40

Count by 15 minutes   4:15

Count by 30 minutes   8:00

Review

Circle the shapes that have 4 right angles.
X the shapes that do not have 4 right angles.

Complete the multiplication table.

×	7	8	9	10
5				
6				
7				
8				
9				

Circle the greatest number in each row.

2,496	2,649	2,600
4,007	4,700	4,707
5,936	3,956	5,639
9,000	8,999	9,001

Solve. Write the equations you use to solve the problems.

Caleb helps his mother build a fence around a square garden. Each side of the garden is 9 feet long. What is the perimeter of the garden?

Mount Rainier is 4,392 meters tall. Mount Hood is 3,429 meters tall. How much taller is Mount Rainier than Mount Hood?

14.2

Lesson Activities 👥

5 past 9	
10 past 9	
quarter past 9	
20 past 9	
25 past 9	
half past 9	

25 to 10	
20 to 10	
quarter to 10	
10 to 10	
5 to 10	
10 o'clock	

Time Riddles

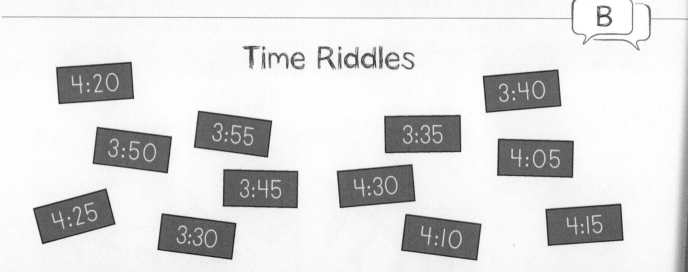

4:20
3:40
3:55
3:35
3:50
4:05
3:45
4:30
4:25
3:30
4:10
4:15

134

Lesson 14.2

Practice 👤 Complete.

half past [ ]

quarter past [ ]

quarter to [ ]

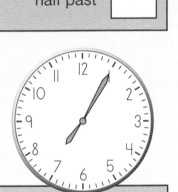

[ ] past [ ]

[ ] past [ ]

[ ] to [ ]

[ ] to [ ]

[ ] past [ ]

[ ] to [ ]

[ ] o'clock

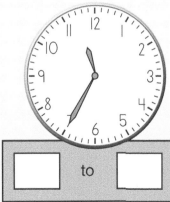

[ ] to [ ]

[ ] past [ ]

14.2

Review   Draw a shape to match each description.

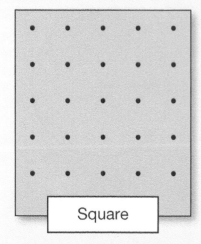

Square

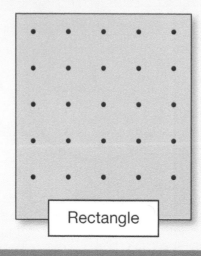

Rectangle

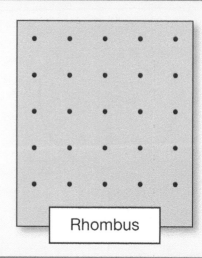

Rhombus

Complete.

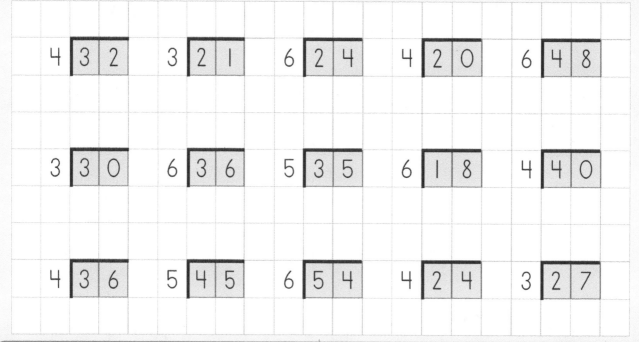

4 3 2	3 2 1	6 2 4	4 2 0	6 4 8
3 3 0	6 3 6	5 3 5	6 1 8	4 4 0
4 3 6	5 4 5	6 5 4	4 2 4	3 2 7

Solve. Write the equations you use to solve the problems.

The bathroom floor is a rectangle
9 feet long and 5 feet wide.
What is the area of the floor?

Evan bought 4 hamburgers and 4 bags
of chips. Each hamburger cost $6, and
each bag of chips cost $2. How much
did he pay?

Lesson Activities 👥

Eleanor's Piano Practice Log

Day	Start Time	End Time	Number of Minutes
Monday	2:20		20
Tuesday	1:35		25
Thursday	3:55		15
Sunday	11:30		60
Monday	1:20	1:35	
Wednesday	2:40	3:00	
Friday	2:40	3:05	
Saturday	12:45	1:45	

Race to 2:00

Player 1	Player 2
12:00	12:00

⚀ = 5 minutes

⚁ = 10 minutes

⚂ = 15 minutes

⚃ = 20 minutes

⚄ = 25 minutes

⚅ = 30 minutes

Practice 👤 Complete.

5:45	**10 min.** ➜	
5:45	**15 min.** ➜	
5:45	**30 min.** ➜	
5:45	**60 min.** ➜	

12:50	**10 min.** ➜	
12:50	**20 min.** ➜	
12:50	**25 min.** ➜	
⭐ 12:50	**42 min.** ➜	

3:55	[ ] min. ➜	4:00
3:55	[ ] min. ➜	4:15
3:55	[ ] min. ➜	4:30
3:55	[ ] min. ➜	4:55

1:20	[ ] min. ➜	1:30
1:20	[ ] min. ➜	2:00
1:20	[ ] min. ➜	2:05
⭐ 1:20	[ ] min. ➜	2:07

Review — Match each word with its definition.

| Square | Rhombus | Rectangle | Quadrilateral |

| 4 equal sides | 4 right angles and 4 equal sides | 4 sides | 4 right angles |

Complete.

5 | 4 | 7

6 | 4 | 0

3 | 2 | 2

4 | 3 | 8

Complete.

1 0 × 8

9 × 8

8 × 8

1 0 × 7

9 × 7

8 × 7

Complete the sequences.

Count by 200s: 7,600, ___, ___, ___, ___, 8,600

Count by 250s: 3,500, ___, ___, ___, ___, 4,750

14.4

Lesson Activities 👥

Gymnastics

- Monday at 2:30

- 20 min. drive

- Leave at ☐

Library Story Hour

- Tuesday at 10:00

- 15 min. bike ride

- Leave at ☐

Dentist Appointment

- Wednesday at 11:10

- 25 min. drive

- Leave at ☐

Visit Aunt Claire

- Thursday at 1:30

- 1 hr. drive

- Leave at ☐

Park Play Date

- Friday at 1:15

- 20 min. walk

- Leave at ☐

B

Race to 12:00

Player 1	Player 2
2:00	2:00

- ⚀ = 5 minutes
- ⚁ = 10 minutes
- ⚂ = 15 minutes
- ⚃ = 20 minutes
- ⚄ = 25 minutes
- ⚅ = 30 minutes

Practice 👤 Complete.

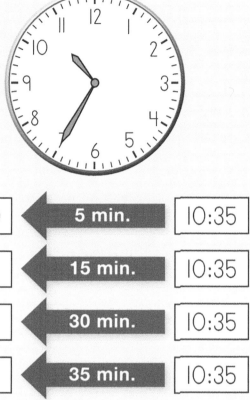

10:30	← 5 min.	10:35
	← 15 min.	10:35
	← 30 min.	10:35
	← 35 min.	10:35

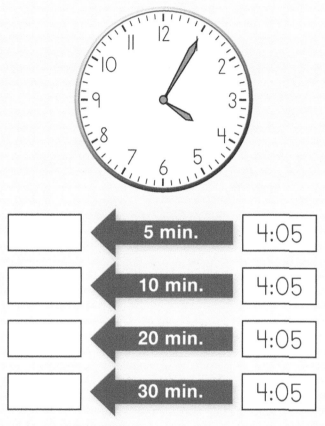

	← 5 min.	4:05
	← 10 min.	4:05
	← 20 min.	4:05
	← 30 min.	4:05

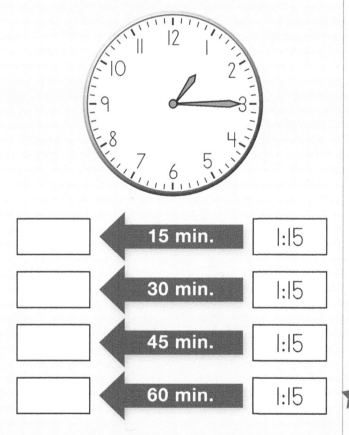

	← 15 min.	1:15
	← 30 min.	1:15
	← 45 min.	1:15
	← 60 min.	1:15

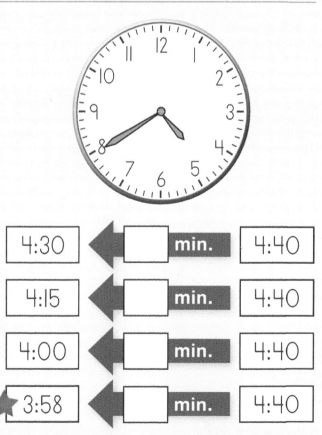

4:30	← ___ min.	4:40
4:15	← ___ min.	4:40
4:00	← ___ min.	4:40
⭐ 3:58	← ___ min.	4:40

14.4

Review   Complete.

36 ÷ 4 = ☐   15 ÷ 3 = ☐   18 ÷ 3 = ☐

24 ÷ 3 = ☐   28 ÷ 4 = ☐   48 ÷ 6 = ☐

60 ÷ 6 = ☐   30 ÷ 6 = ☐   32 ÷ 4 = ☐

Complete.

3,900 + 400 = ☐   3,200 - 2,000 = ☐

4,500 + 2,000 = ☐   3,790 - 10 = ☐

3,150 + 50 = ☐   5,000 - 4,500 = ☐

7,290 + 400 = ☐   3,900 - 3,600 = ☐

Solve. Write the equations you use to solve the problems.

Veronica is making bracelets. She has 42 beads. If she puts 6 beads on each bracelet, how many bracelets can she make?

Veronica is making bracelets. She has 42 beads. If she puts 10 beads on each bracelet, how many bracelets can she make?

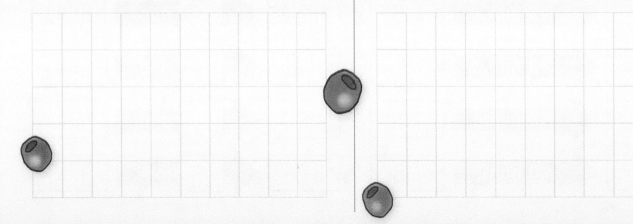

Lesson Activities 👥

A

Multiplication Undercover

Player 1	8	16	24	32	40	48	56	64	72	80
Player 2	8	16	24	32	40	48	56	64	72	80

B

Day Camp Schedule

Activity	Start Time	End Time
Outdoor Skills (1 hr. 10 min.)	8:00	
Capture the Flag (1 hr. 15 min.)		
Hike (1 hr. 45 min.)		
Lunch and Sing-along (50 min.)		
Afternoon Choice Time (3 hr. 30 min.)		

AFTERNOON ACTIVITY CHOICES

Activity	Start Time	End Time	Length of Activity
Swimming	1:00	4:00	
Canoeing	2:30	4:30	
Archery	2:00	3:40	
Crafts	1:30	2:45	
Rock Climbing	2:45	4:25	

Practice 👤 Complete.

9:00	1 hr. →	
9:00	2 hr. →	
9:00	2 hr. 45 min. →	
9:00	3 hr. 20 min. →	

2:45	2 hr. →	
2:45	2 hr. 10 min. →	
2:45	2 hr. 15 min. →	
2:45	2 hr. 25 min. →	

6:00	☐ hr. →	8:00
6:00	☐ hr. ☐ min. →	8:30
6:00	☐ hr. ☐ min. →	9:40
6:00	☐ hr. →	12:00

4:50	☐ hr. →	6:50
4:50	☐ hr. ☐ min. →	7:00
★ 4:50	☐ hr. ☐ min. →	7:15
★ 4:50	☐ hr. ☐ min. →	8:05

Review

Round to the nearest thousand.

5,450	6,975	1,050	8,350	4,625	7,250

Match each shape to its name.

 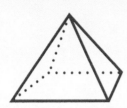 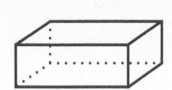  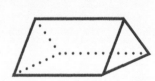

Pyramid	Triangular prism	Cylinder	Rectangular prism	Cone

Complete.

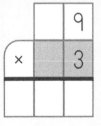

Row 1:

	9		8		9		4		8
×	3	×	5	×	7	×	7	×	6

Row 2:

	8		8		6		9		8
×	8	×	3	×	7	×	4	×	7

Row 3:

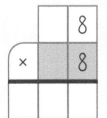

	9		5		9		7		8
×	8	×	7	×	6	×	7	×	4

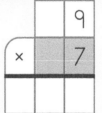 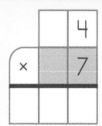

Lesson Activities 👥

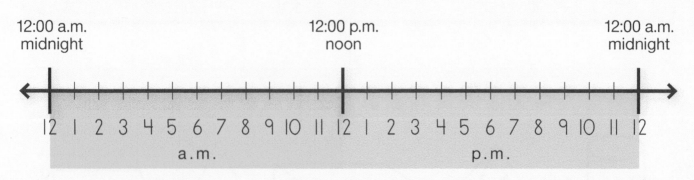

12:00 a.m.
midnight

12:00 p.m.
noon

12:00 a.m.
midnight

12 1 2 3 4 5 6 7 8 9 10 11 12 1 2 3 4 5 6 7 8 9 10 11 12

a.m.

p.m.

Time	How Long Until Midnight?	Time	How Long After Midnight?
7:00 p.m.		12:30 a.m.	
8:00 p.m.		1:00 a.m.	
8:30 p.m.		1:45 a.m.	
9:45 p.m.		2:00 a.m.	
10:00 p.m.		2:45 a.m.	
11:30 p.m.		3:30 a.m.	

Practice 👤   Complete. Use the timeline to help.

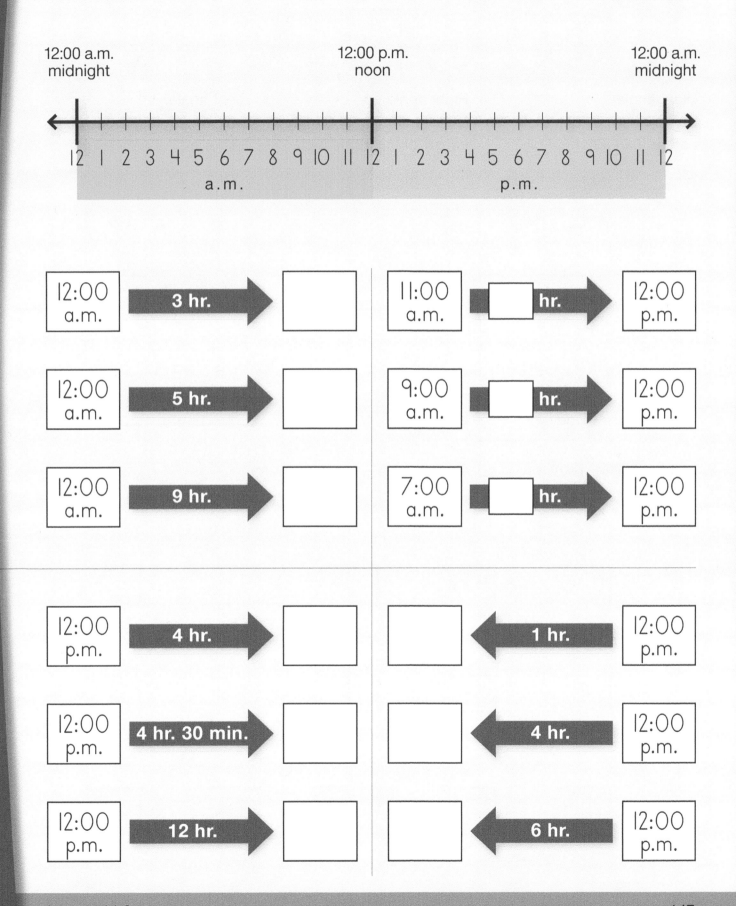

12:00 a.m.
midnight

12:00 p.m.
noon

12:00 a.m.
midnight

12 1 2 3 4 5 6 7 8 9 10 11 12 1 2 3 4 5 6 7 8 9 10 11 12

a.m.

p.m.

| 12:00 a.m. | → 3 hr. | ☐ | | 11:00 a.m. | → ☐ hr. | 12:00 p.m. |

| 12:00 a.m. | → 5 hr. | ☐ | | 9:00 a.m. | → ☐ hr. | 12:00 p.m. |

| 12:00 a.m. | → 9 hr. | ☐ | | 7:00 a.m. | → ☐ hr. | 12:00 p.m. |

| 12:00 p.m. | → 4 hr. | ☐ | | ☐ | ← 1 hr. | 12:00 p.m. |

| 12:00 p.m. | → 4 hr. 30 min. | ☐ | | ☐ | ← 4 hr. | 12:00 p.m. |

| 12:00 p.m. | → 12 hr. | ☐ | | ☐ | ← 6 hr. | 12:00 p.m. |

Review 👤 Circle the description that matches the angle.

Right angle
Smaller than a right angle
Larger than a right angle

Right angle
Smaller than a right angle
Larger than a right angle

Right angle
Smaller than a right angle
Larger than a right angle

Complete.

6 weeks = [ ] days

7 weeks = [ ] days

8 weeks = [ ] days

6 weeks, 3 days = [ ] days

7 weeks, 1 day = [ ] days

8 weeks, 4 days = [ ] days

Complete.

```
  3 , 0 0 0
-   1 , 7 4 2
_____
```

```
  5 , 6 9 4
+       5 3 6
_____
```

Complete.

3 ⟌ 3 0   6 ⟌ 4 2   4 ⟌ 2 8   4 ⟌ 2 0   3 ⟌ 2 7

6 ⟌ 6 0   3 ⟌ 2 1   6 ⟌ 4 8   3 ⟌ 1 8   4 ⟌ 3 6

4 ⟌ 2 4   6 ⟌ 5 4   3 ⟌ 2 4   4 ⟌ 4 0   6 ⟌ 3 6

Lesson Activities 👥

| 12:00 a.m. midnight | | | | | | | | | | | | 12:00 p.m. noon | | | | | | | | | | | | 12:00 a.m. midnight |

12 1 2 3 4 5 6 7 8 9 10 11 12 1 2 3 4 5 6 7 8 9 10 11 12

a.m.   p.m.

B

Animal Shelter Volunteer Log

Start Time	End Time	Elapsed Time
11:00 a.m.		2 hr. 45 min.
11:30 a.m.	2:00 p.m.	
	3:45 p.m.	2 hr. 15 min.
12:00 p.m.		4 hr. 20 min.
3:30 p.m.	7:15 p.m.	
	6:05 p.m.	2 hr. 30 min.
8:00 p.m.	8:00 a.m.	
9:30 p.m.		9 hr. 45 min.

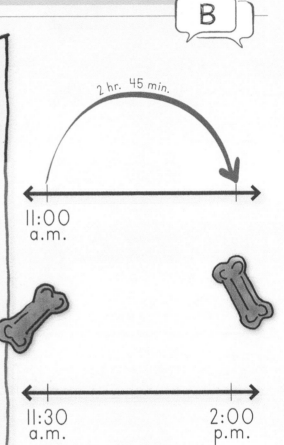

2 hr. 45 min.

11:00 a.m.

11:30 a.m.   2:00 p.m.

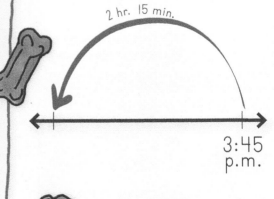

2 hr. 15 min.

3:45 p.m.

Practice 👤 Complete. Use the timelines to help.

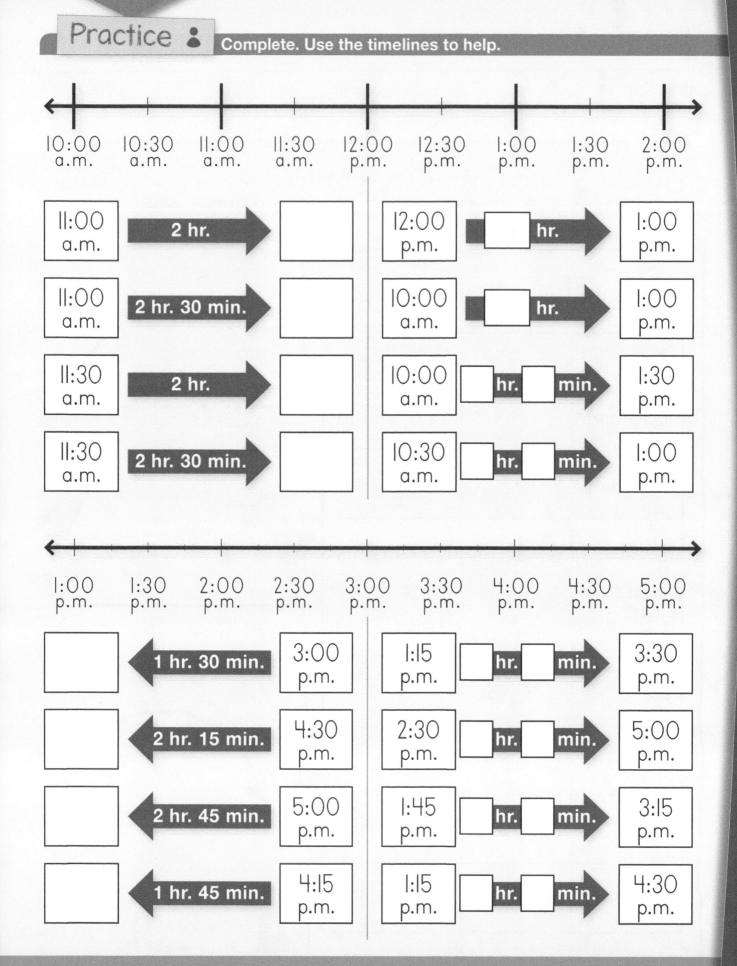

Review

Complete. Follow the steps.

1. Divide
2. Multiply
3. Subtract

| 5 | 3 | 1 | | 4 | 2 | 5 | | 3 | 1 | 9 | | 1 | 0 | 6 | 1 |

Complete.

360 + 60 = ☐

480 + 60 = ☐

600 - 60 = ☐

7 × 60 = ☐

8 × 60 = ☐

9 × 60 = ☐

Complete the charts to match the shapes.

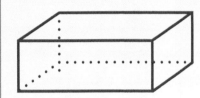

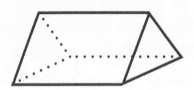

Faces	
Edges	
Vertices	

Faces	
Edges	
Vertices	

Solve. Write the equations you use to solve the problems.

Arjun helps his parents plant 90 carrot seeds. They plant 9 rows.
How many seeds are in each row?

Arjun helps his parents plant flowers, too. They plant 6 rows.
They plant 20 flowers in each row.
How many flowers do they plant?

Lesson Activities 👥

Elapsed Time Tic-Tac-Toe

Start	End
7:00	9:30
7:15	9:45
7:30	10:00
7:45	10:15
8:00	10:30
8:15	10:45

All times are a.m.

2 hr. 45 min.	3 hr. 15 min.	1 hr. 30 min.	2 hr. 30 min.
3 hr.	2 hr.	2 hr. 45 min.	3 hr. 30 min.
2 hr. 30 min.	1 hr. 45 min.	2 hr.	1 hr. 15 min.
3 hr. 45 min.	2 hr. 15 min.	3 hr.	2 hr. 15 min.

Ruby starts watching a movie at 1:45 p.m.
The movie is 2 hours and 20 minutes long.
When will the movie be over?

The baby naps from 12:50 p.m. until
2:40 p.m. How long does the baby nap?

Jayden's family is making a ham.
They want the ham to be done at 1:15 p.m.
The ham takes 2 hours and 40 minutes
to bake. When should they put the ham
in the oven?

Practice 👤 Complete. Use the timeline sketches to help.

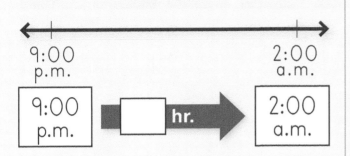

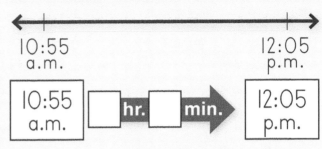

Solve.

The plane takes off at 9:30 a.m. and lands at 1:15 p.m. How long is the flight?

It takes 2 hours and 35 minutes to get to Charlie's cousins' house. If his family starts driving at 3:45 p.m., when will they arrive?

Quinn's baseball game lasted 1 hour and 40 minutes. It ended at 8:20 p.m. When did the game begin?

 Brynn wants to get 10 hours of sleep. If she goes to bed at 8:30 p.m., when should she wake up?

Review 👤 Use the numbers to complete the blanks. You will use each number once.

| 1 | 2 | 3 | 4 | 5 | 6 | 7 | 8 | 9 |

☐ × 7 = 14   7 × ☐ = 28   7 × ☐ = 49

☐ × 7 = 56   7 × ☐ = 7   7 × ☐ = 21

☐ × 7 = 35   7 × ☐ = 63   7 × ☐ = 42

Complete.

$

$

Complete.

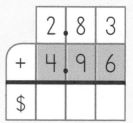

```
  2 . 8  3
+ 4 . 9  6
$
```

```
  9 . 1  5
- 5 . 4  7
$
```

Complete the sequences.

★ 6,250 + 1,275 = ☐   ★ 4,700 − 1,250 = ☐

6,250 + 1,250 = ☐   4,700 − 1,200 = ☐

Start 6,250 + 1,000 = ☐   4,700 − 1,000 = ☐

Unit Wrap-Up 👤   Write the time.

   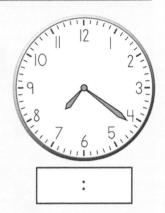

| : | : | : | : |

Match.

quarter to 8		7:45
quarter past 8		7:50
10 to 8		8:10
10 past 8		8:15
half past 8		8:30

Write a.m. or p.m. for each meal.

Breakfast	Morning Snack
7:30 ☐	10:15 ☐
Lunch	Afternoon Snack
12:00 ☐	3:45 ☐
Dinner	Midnight Snack
6:15 ☐	12:00 ☐

Complete.

7:25	→ 20 min. →	☐		☐	← 10 min. ←	8:15
7:25	→ 35 min. →	☐		☐	← 20 min. ←	8:15
7:25	→ 2 hr. →	☐		☐	← 3 hr. ←	8:15
7:25	→ 2 hr. 30 min. →	☐		☐	← 3 hr. 20 min. ←	8:15

Unit Wrap-Up

Complete. Make sure to write a.m. or p.m. for each time.

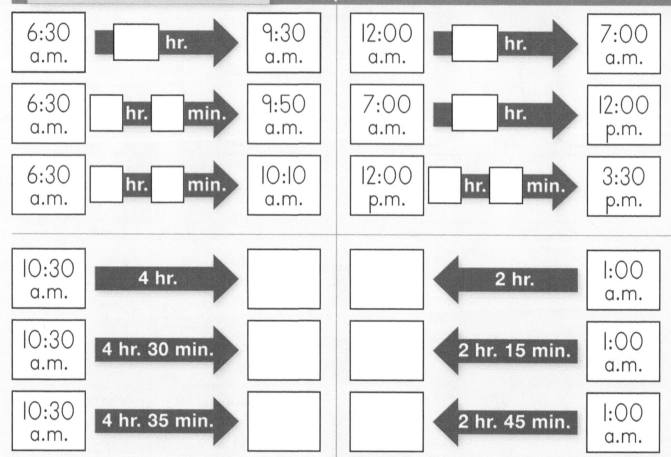

6:30 a.m.	☐ hr. →	9:30 a.m.	12:00 a.m.	☐ hr. →	7:00 a.m.
6:30 a.m.	☐ hr. ☐ min. →	9:50 a.m.	7:00 a.m.	☐ hr. →	12:00 p.m.
6:30 a.m.	☐ hr. ☐ min. →	10:10 a.m.	12:00 p.m.	☐ hr. ☐ min. →	3:30 p.m.

10:30 a.m.	4 hr. →	☐	☐	← 2 hr.	1:00 a.m.
10:30 a.m.	4 hr. 30 min. →	☐	☐	← 2 hr. 15 min.	1:00 a.m.
10:30 a.m.	4 hr. 35 min. →	☐	☐	← 2 hr. 45 min.	1:00 a.m.

Solve.

Karate class is 50 minutes long. It ends at 4:30 p.m. When does karate class begin?

Ramona played outside from 2:30 p.m. to 4:40 p.m. How long did she play outside?

The movie was 2 hours and 5 minutes long. It ended at 1:25 p.m. When did the movie begin?

Xavier's grandparents are coming to visit. At 9:25 a.m., they called to say they have 1 hour and 50 minutes left to drive. When will they arrive?

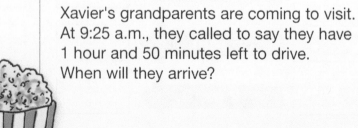

Lesson Activities 👥

$56 \div 7 = \boxed{}$

$\boxed{} \times 7 = 56$

$14 \div 7 = \boxed{}$ $28 \div 7 = \boxed{}$ $35 \div 7 = \boxed{}$

$42 \div 7 = \boxed{}$ $7 \div 7 = \boxed{}$ $49 \div 7 = \boxed{}$

$21 \div 7 = \boxed{}$ $70 \div 7 = \boxed{}$ $63 \div 7 = \boxed{}$

Dice Tic-Tac-Toe

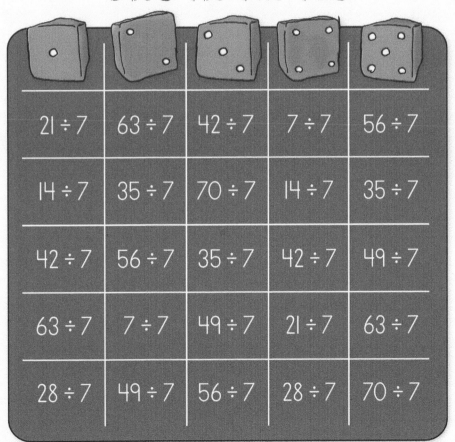

$21 \div 7$	$63 \div 7$	$42 \div 7$	$7 \div 7$	$56 \div 7$
$14 \div 7$	$35 \div 7$	$70 \div 7$	$14 \div 7$	$35 \div 7$
$42 \div 7$	$56 \div 7$	$35 \div 7$	$42 \div 7$	$49 \div 7$
$63 \div 7$	$7 \div 7$	$49 \div 7$	$21 \div 7$	$63 \div 7$
$28 \div 7$	$49 \div 7$	$56 \div 7$	$28 \div 7$	$70 \div 7$

Practice 👤   Complete and match the equations.

☐ × 7 = 14	42 ÷ 7 = ☐
☐ × 7 = 28	49 ÷ 7 = ☐
☐ × 7 = 42	14 ÷ 7 = ☐
☐ × 7 = 35	70 ÷ 7 = ☐
☐ × 7 = 49	28 ÷ 7 = ☐
☐ × 7 = 7	35 ÷ 7 = ☐
☐ × 7 = 70	7 ÷ 7 = ☐
☐ × 7 = 63	56 ÷ 7 = ☐
☐ × 7 = 21	63 ÷ 7 = ☐
☐ × 7 = 56	21 ÷ 7 = ☐

Review · Complete the two missing sides for each square.

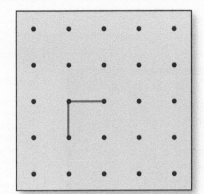 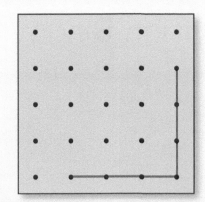 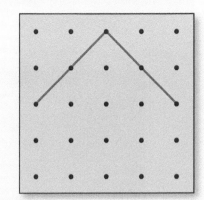

Complete.

$24 \div 3 =$ ☐

$25 \div 3 =$ ☐

$26 \div 3 =$ ☐

$27 \div 3 =$ ☐

Complete.

4 weeks = ☐ days

4 weeks, 2 days = ☐ days

7 weeks = ☐ days

7 weeks, 6 days = ☐ days

Use logical thinking to label the missing sides.

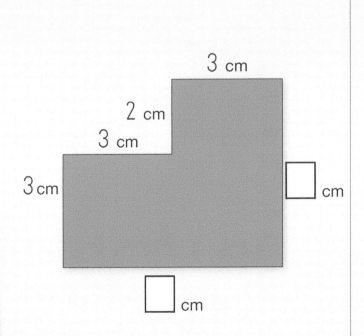

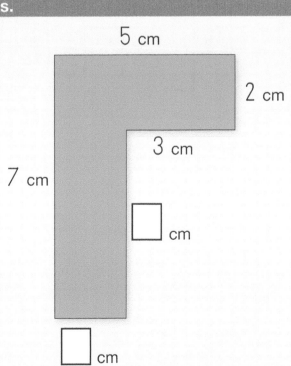

Lesson Activities 👥

Division Bingo (÷7)

B	I	N	G	O
35	28	56	14	63
70	49	42	21	42
7	63	70	28	56
49	21	42	49	70
56	35	14	63	7

B	I	N	G	O
14	7	49	63	70
42	35	56	28	7
70	63	21	42	49
42	56	14	28	70
21	49	63	56	35

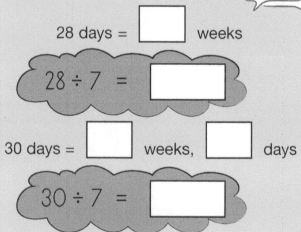

28 days = ☐ weeks

28 ÷ 7 = ☐

30 days = ☐ weeks, ☐ days

30 ÷ 7 = ☐

14 days = ☐ weeks

17 days = ☐ weeks, ☐ days

49 days = ☐ weeks

50 days = ☐ weeks, ☐ days

Practice

Complete.

| 7 | 7 | 0 | | 7 | 6 | 3 | | 7 | 2 | 8 | | 7 | 5 | 6 | | 7 | 2 | 1 |

| 7 | 1 | 4 | | 7 | 4 | 9 | | 7 | 3 | 5 | | 7 | 4 | 2 | | 7 | 7 | |

| 5 | 4 | 0 | | 6 | 4 | 8 | | 4 | 3 | 2 | | 3 | 2 | 4 | | 2 | 1 | 6 |

| 3 | 2 | 7 | | 5 | 4 | 5 | | 2 | 1 | 8 | | 6 | 5 | 4 | | 4 | 3 | 6 |

Complete.

21 days = ☐ weeks

27 days = ☐ weeks, ☐ days

35 days = ☐ weeks

40 days = ☐ weeks, ☐ days

70 days = ☐ weeks

71 days = ☐ weeks, ☐ days

★ 77 days = ☐ weeks

80 days = ☐ weeks, ☐ days

Review 👤
Color the multiples in order from Start to End.

Complete.

Multiples of 8

50	54	56	64	72
45	49	48	63	80
14	10	40	42	81
12	20	32	36	28
8	16	24	35	21

END

Start →

$30 \times 5 =$ ☐

$20 \times 7 =$ ☐

$50 \times 6 =$ ☐

$90 \times 2 =$ ☐

$18 \times 10 =$ ☐

Complete. Use the timeline sketches to help.

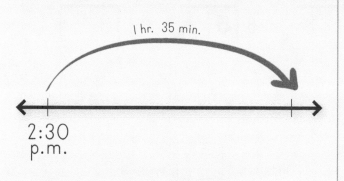

1 hr. 35 min.

2:30 p.m.

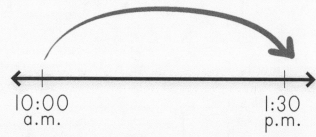

10:00 a.m.

1:30 p.m.

 2:30 p.m. **1 hr. 35 min.** →

 10:00 a.m. ☐ **hr.** ☐ **min.** → 1:30 p.m.

Complete the two missing sides for each rhombus.

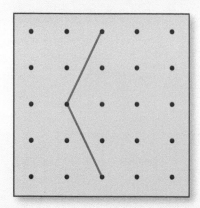

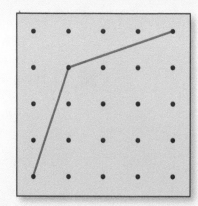

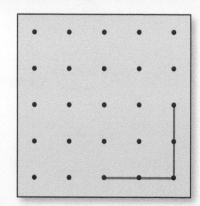

Lesson Activities 👥

A

$64 \div 8 = \boxed{}$

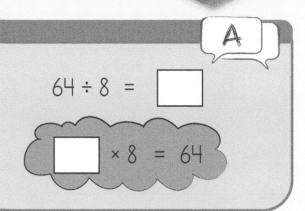

$\boxed{} \times 8 = 64$

$24 \div 8 = \boxed{}$ $32 \div 8 = \boxed{}$ $80 \div 8 = \boxed{}$

$56 \div 8 = \boxed{}$ $16 \div 8 = \boxed{}$ $72 \div 8 = \boxed{}$

$40 \div 8 = \boxed{}$ $48 \div 8 = \boxed{}$ $8 \div 8 = \boxed{}$

B

Climb and Slide

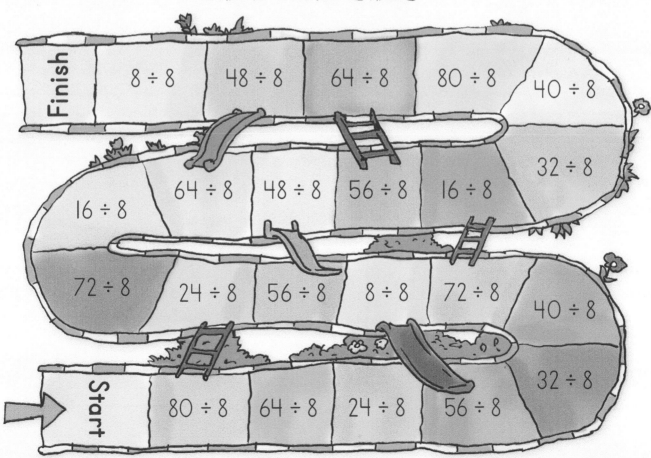

Practice 👤 Complete and match the equations.

☐ × 8 = 24	24 ÷ 8 = ☐
☐ × 8 = 40	80 ÷ 8 = ☐
☐ × 8 = 32	8 ÷ 8 = ☐
☐ × 8 = 8	32 ÷ 8 = ☐
☐ × 8 = 48	40 ÷ 8 = ☐
☐ × 8 = 80	56 ÷ 8 = ☐
☐ × 8 = 56	72 ÷ 8 = ☐
☐ × 8 = 64	64 ÷ 8 = ☐
☐ × 8 = 72	16 ÷ 8 = ☐
☐ × 8 = 16	48 ÷ 8 = ☐

Review 👤 Find the perimeter of each shape.

Each side is 5 ft. long.

Perimeter: _____

Each side is 3 m long.

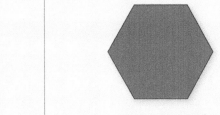

Perimeter: _____

Each side is 4 yd. long.

Perimeter: _____

Complete the sequences.

Count by
25 minutes — 7:30

Count by
30 minutes — 8:55

Count by
45 minutes — 4:30

Solve.

Daniela played with blocks for 1 hour and 20 minutes. She started at 3:50 p.m. When did she end?

Daniela stacked the blocks to make a wall. She used 36 blocks and arranged them in 4 equal rows. How many blocks were in each row?

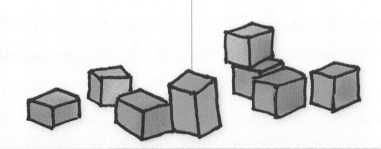

Lesson Activities 👥

Division Crash (÷8)

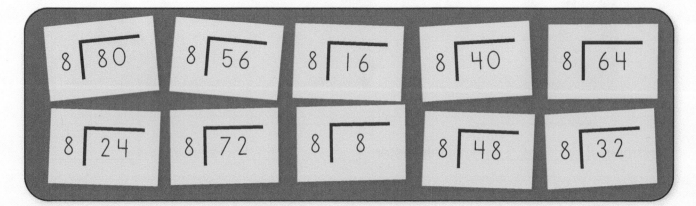

8) 80   8) 56   8) 16   8) 40   8) 64

8) 24   8) 72   8) 8   8) 48   8) 32

Perimeter: 15 cm

Length of each side: ____

All sides are equal.

Perimeter: 20 yd.

Length of each side: ____

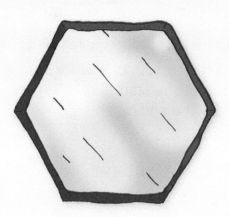

Perimeter: 54 in.

Length of each side: ____

Practice 👤 Complete.

$40 \div 8 =$ ☐ $48 \div 8 =$ ☐ $16 \div 8 =$ ☐

$24 \div 8 =$ ☐ $64 \div 8 =$ ☐ $56 \div 8 =$ ☐

$72 \div 8 =$ ☐ $80 \div 8 =$ ☐ $32 \div 8 =$ ☐

$56 \div 7 =$ ☐ $32 \div 4 =$ ☐ $48 \div 6 =$ ☐

Complete. The sides of each shape are the same length.

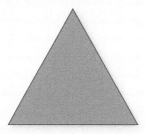

Perimeter: 27 in.

Length of each side: ☐

Perimeter: 28 m

Length of each side: ☐

Perimeter: 80 cm

Length of each side: ☐

Perimeter: 40 ft.

Length of each side: ☐

Review

Circle the more sensible unit for each item.

Area of a computer screen

150 sq. ft.	150 sq. in.

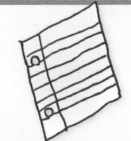

Area of a piece of paper

600 sq. m	600 sq. cm

Area of a poster

1 sq. mi.	1 sq. yd.

Color the multiples in order from Start to End.

Multiples of 9

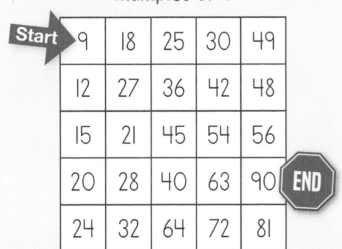

Start →

9	18	25	30	49
12	27	36	42	48
15	21	45	54	56
20	28	40	63	90	END
24	32	64	72	81

Complete.

$10 \times 5 + 3 =$ ☐

$7 \times 4 + 2 =$ ☐

$9 \times 3 + 6 =$ ☐

$5 \times 8 + 4 =$ ☐

$6 \times 4 + 1 =$ ☐

Complete. Use the timeline sketch to help.

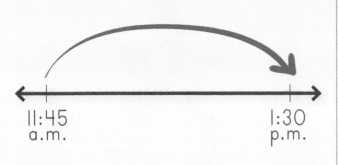

11:45 a.m.   1:30 p.m.

| 11:45 a.m. | ☐ hr. ☐ min. → | 1:30 p.m. |

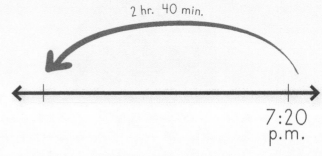

2 hr. 40 min.

7:20 p.m.

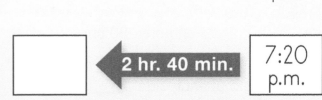

| ☐ | ← 2 hr. 40 min. | 7:20 p.m. |

Lesson Activities

A

$36 \div 9 = \boxed{}$

$\boxed{} \times 9 = 36$

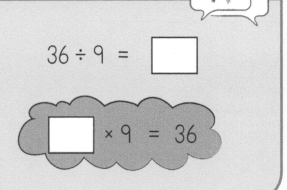

$18 \div 9 = \boxed{}$ $90 \div 9 = \boxed{}$ $72 \div 9 = \boxed{}$

$81 \div 9 = \boxed{}$ $9 \div 9 = \boxed{}$ $63 \div 9 = \boxed{}$

$27 \div 9 = \boxed{}$ $45 \div 9 = \boxed{}$ $54 \div 9 = \boxed{}$

B

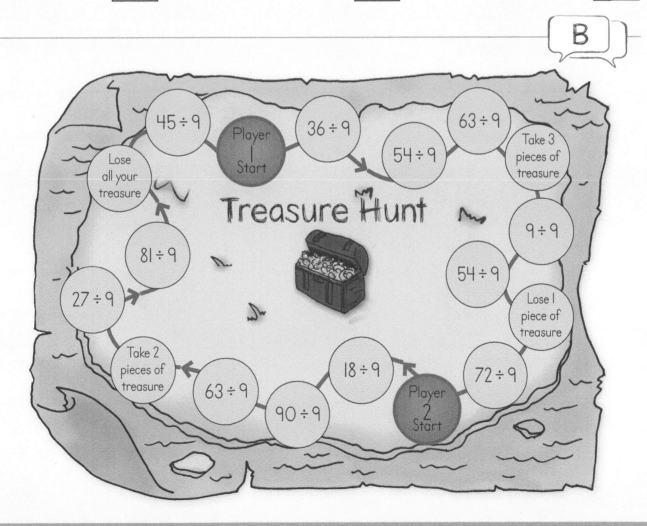

Practice 👤 Complete and match the equations.

$\boxed{} \times 9 = 9$	$90 \div 9 = \boxed{}$
$\boxed{} \times 9 = 90$	$81 \div 9 = \boxed{}$
$\boxed{} \times 9 = 81$	$45 \div 9 = \boxed{}$
$\boxed{} \times 9 = 18$	$9 \div 9 = \boxed{}$
$\boxed{} \times 9 = 45$	$72 \div 9 = \boxed{}$
$\boxed{} \times 9 = 72$	$18 \div 9 = \boxed{}$
$\boxed{} \times 9 = 54$	$36 \div 9 = \boxed{}$
$\boxed{} \times 9 = 27$	$54 \div 9 = \boxed{}$
$\boxed{} \times 9 = 36$	$27 \div 9 = \boxed{}$
$\boxed{} \times 9 = 63$	$63 \div 9 = \boxed{}$

Review 👤 Write a fact family to match the array.

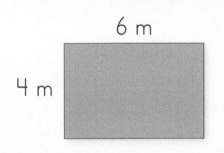

3	×	8	=	
	×		=	
	÷		=	
	÷		=	

Find the area.

6 m

4 m

Area: ____

2 ft.

3 ft.

Area: ____

10 in.

10 in.

Area: ____

Complete.

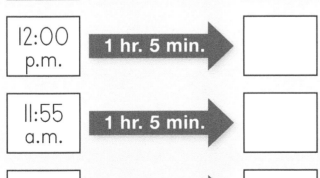

12:05 p.m.	**1 hr. 5 min.** →	
12:00 p.m.	**1 hr. 5 min.** →	
11:55 a.m.	**1 hr. 5 min.** →	
11:50 a.m.	**1 hr. 5 min.** →	

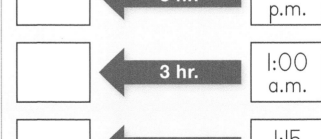

	← **3 hr.**	7:00 p.m.
	← **3 hr.**	7:20 p.m.
	← **3 hr.**	1:00 a.m.
	← **3 hr.**	1:15 a.m.

Lesson Activities

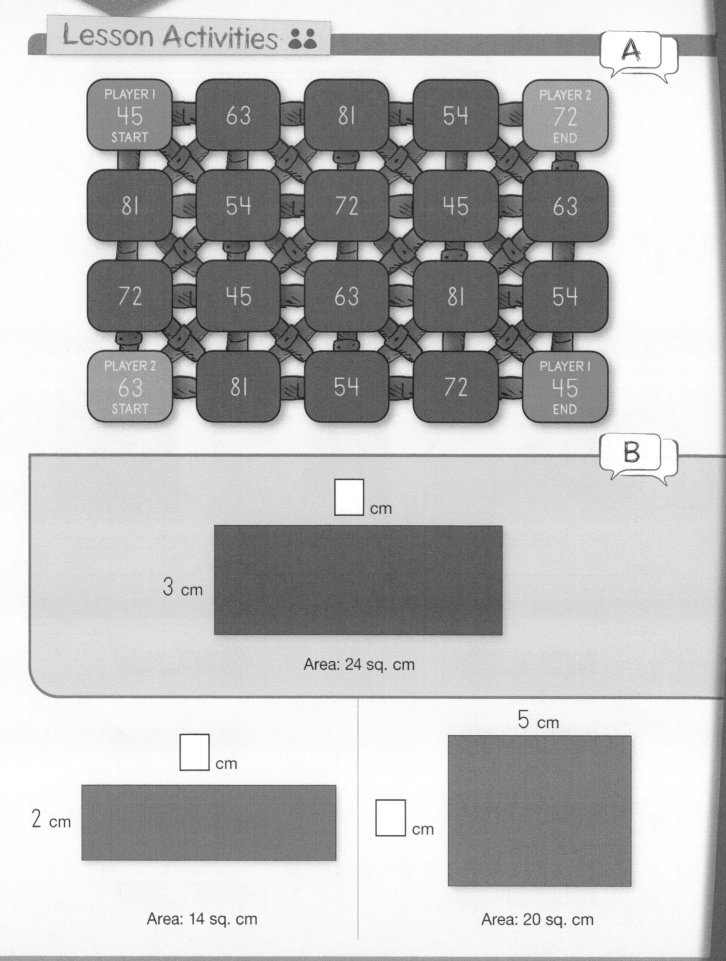

A

PLAYER 1 45 START	63	81	54	PLAYER 2 72 END
81	54	72	45	63
72	45	63	81	54
PLAYER 2 63 START	81	54	72	PLAYER 1 45 END

B

☐ cm

3 cm

Area: 24 sq. cm

☐ cm

2 cm

Area: 14 sq. cm

5 cm

☐ cm

Area: 20 sq. cm

Practice 👤 Complete.

90 ÷ 9 = ☐   81 ÷ 9 = ☐   45 ÷ 9 = ☐

54 ÷ 9 = ☐   18 ÷ 9 = ☐   72 ÷ 9 = ☐

36 ÷ 9 = ☐   63 ÷ 9 = ☐   27 ÷ 9 = ☐

63 ÷ 7 = ☐   72 ÷ 8 = ☐   54 ÷ 6 = ☐

Complete.

☐ ft.

2 ft.

Area: 6 sq. ft.

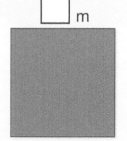
☐ m

5 m

Area: 25 sq. m

7 cm

☐ cm

Area: 35 sq. cm

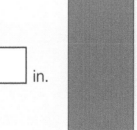
4 in.

☐ in.

Area: 32 sq. in.

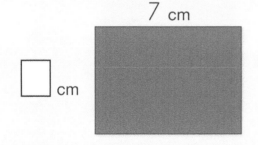
☐ yd.

1 yd.

Area: 9 sq. yd.

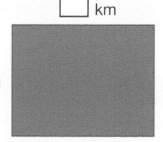
☐ km

3 km

Area: 12 sq. km

Review 👤 Complete.

past	to	quarter to

Use a ruler to measure each line to the nearest quarter inch.

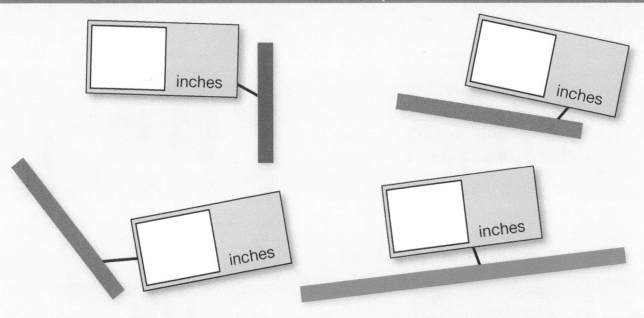

inches

inches

inches

inches

Solve.

David's family arrived at the fair at 10:45 a.m. They left at 2:05 p.m. How long did they spend at the fair?

David's family bought 6 sandwiches for $8 each. They bought 6 ice cream cones for $3 each. How much more did they spend on sandwiches than ice cream cones?

Unit Wrap-Up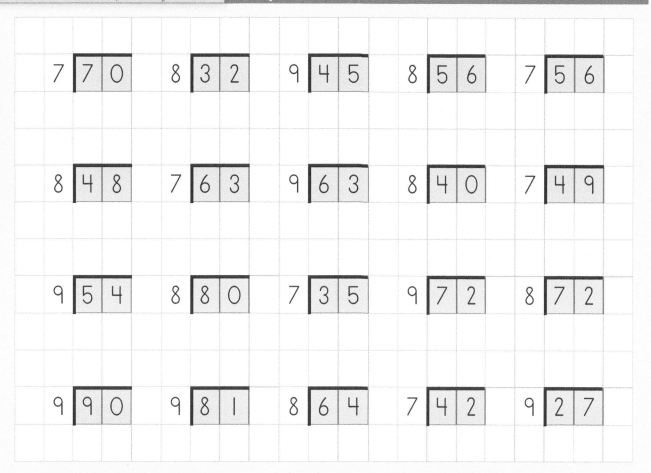

Complete.

7	7	0		8	3	2		9	4	5		8	5	6		7	5	6
8	4	8		7	6	3		9	6	3		8	4	0		7	4	9
9	5	4		8	8	0		7	3	5		9	7	2		8	7	2
9	9	0		9	8	1		8	6	4		7	4	2		9	2	7

Complete.

14 days = ☐ weeks

20 days = ☐ weeks, ☐ days

42 days = ☐ weeks

45 days = ☐ weeks, ☐ days

28 days = ☐ weeks

31 days = ☐ weeks, ☐ days

56 days = ☐ weeks

61 days = ☐ weeks, ☐ days

Unit Wrap-Up 👤 **Complete.**

All sides are equal.

Perimeter: 32 ft.

Length of each side: _____

All sides are equal.

Perimeter: 24 m

Length of each side: _____

6 cm

☐ cm

Area: 36 sq. cm

☐ in.

5 in.

Area: 45 sq. in.

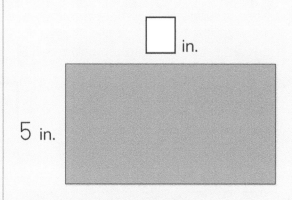

Solve. Write the equations you use to solve the problems.

RJ arranges his rock collection in bins. He has 72 rocks. 9 rocks fit in each bin. How many bins does he fill?

Audrey organizes her stuffed animals on shelves. She has 56 stuffed animals and 8 shelves. She puts the same number on each shelf. How many stuffed animals are on each shelf?

Lesson Activities 👥

| ounce (oz.) | 16 ounces = | pound | | pound (lb.)

Item	Estimated Weight	Actual Weight

Practice

Choose the more sensible unit for each item.

Weight of a dumbbell

5	5
oz.	lb.

Weight of an egg

2	2
oz.	lb.

Weight of a new baby

8	8
oz.	lb.

Find the weight of each item. Include the correct unit.

Solve. Write the equations you use to solve the problems.

Bella's grandma needs 32 oz. of tomatoes for a recipe. Each tomato weighs about 4 oz. How many tomatoes does she need?

The mother elephant at the zoo weighs 6,507 lb. Her baby weighs 237 lb. How much more does the mother elephant weigh than her baby?

Caleb has 48 oz. of modeling clay. He splits the clay equally into 8 balls. How much does each ball weigh?

Oliver weighs 72 lb. His little sister weighs 34 lb. less than him. How much does his sister weigh?

Review 👤 Match.

90 ÷ 9		6		72 ÷ 8
72 ÷ 9		7		56 ÷ 8
54 ÷ 9		8		48 ÷ 8
81 ÷ 9		9		80 ÷ 8
63 ÷ 9		10		64 ÷ 8

Complete.

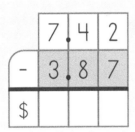

```
    7 . 4  2
-   3 . 8  7
$
```

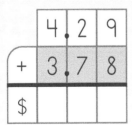

```
    4 . 2  9
+   3 . 7  8
$
```

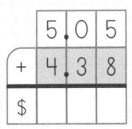

```
    5 . 0  5
+   4 . 3  8
$
```

Complete. Use long division.

```
9 ) 6 7       8 ) 7 0       7 ) 7 3
```

Complete.

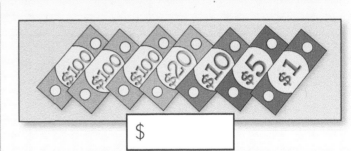

$100 $100 $100 $20 $10 $5 $1

$

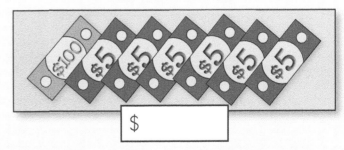

$100 $5 $5 $5 $5 $5 $5

$

16.2

Lesson Activities 👥

A

| gram (g) | **1,000 grams = 1 kilogram** | 1 kilogram (kg) |

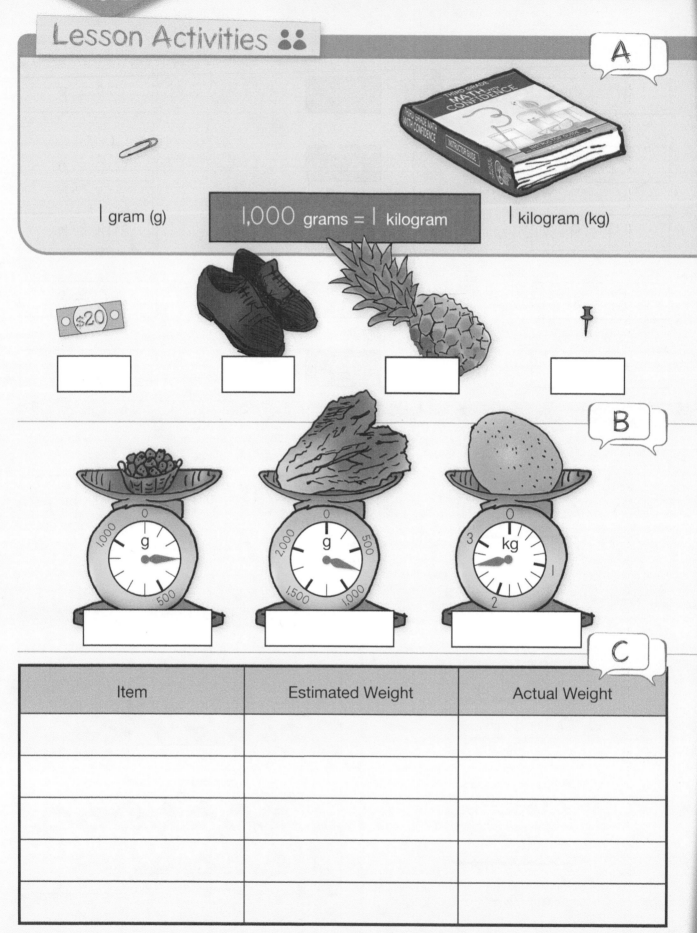

$20

B

g   g   kg

C

Item	Estimated Weight	Actual Weight

Practice

Choose the more sensible unit for each item.

Weight of a dumbbell

2 g	2 kg

Weight of an egg

60 g	60 kg

Weight of a new baby

4 g	4 kg

Find the weight of each item. Include the correct unit.

Solve. Write the equations you use to solve the problems.

Eve weighs 29 kg.
Her brother weighs 16 kg more than her.
How much does her brother weigh?

The baby horse weighs 48 kg.
Its mother weighs 512 kg. How much less does the baby weigh than its mother?

Ana has 7 balls of modeling clay.
Each ball weighs 80 g. If she puts the clay together into one big ball, how much will the ball weigh?

The bread recipe calls for 275 g of white flour and 175 g of whole wheat flour. How many total grams of flour are in the recipe?

16.2

Review **Match.**

70 ÷ 7	6	48 ÷ 6
42 ÷ 7	7	36 ÷ 6
63 ÷ 7	8	60 ÷ 6
49 ÷ 7	9	42 ÷ 6
56 ÷ 7	10	54 ÷ 6

Complete.

All sides are equal.

Perimeter: 42 m

Length of each side: _____

All sides are equal.

Perimeter: 36 in.

Length of each side: _____

Complete.

4:45 →15 min.→ _____   _____ ←35 min.← 6:30

2:55 →25 min.→ _____   _____ ←20 min.← 7:10

3:05 →30 min.→ _____   _____ ←30 min.← 8:45

10:40 →40 min.→ _____   _____ ←25 min.← 9:05

Lesson Activities 👥

A

1 cup (c.)　　1 pint (pt.)　　1 quart (qt.)　　1 gallon (gal.)

B

 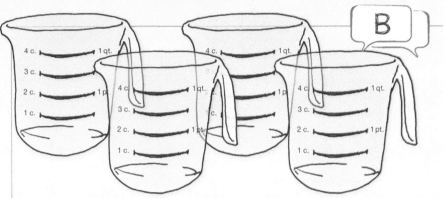

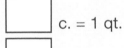

☐ c. = 1 pt.

☐ c. = 1 qt.

☐ pt. = 1 qt.

4 qt. = 1 gal.

⭐ ☐ c. = 1 gal.

⭐ ☐ pt. = 1 gal.

C

Capacity Scavenger Hunt

Holds less than 1 cup

Holds more than 1 cup and less than 1 pint

Holds more than 1 pint and less than 1 quart

Holds more than 1 quart and less than 1 gallon

Holds more than 1 gallon

Practice 👤 Choose the more sensible unit for each item.

Capacity of a bathtub

42 c.	42 gal.

Capacity of a teapot

3 c.	3 gal.

Capacity of an aquarium

10 c.	10 gal.

Complete with <, >, or =.

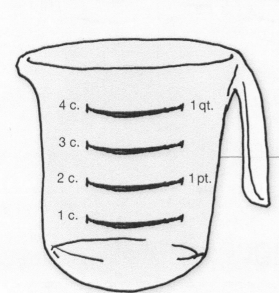

4 c. — 1 qt.
3 c.
2 c. — 1 pt.
1 c.

1 c. ◯ 1 pt.

2 c. ◯ 1 pt.

3 c. ◯ 1 pt.

1 pt. ◯ 1 qt.

2 pt. ◯ 1 qt.

3 pt. ◯ 1 qt.

2 c. ◯ 1 qt.

3 c. ◯ 1 qt.

4 c. ◯ 1 qt.

★ 5 c. ◯ 1 qt.

★ 3 qt. ◯ 12 c.

★ 8 pt. ◯ 5 qt.

Solve. Write the equations you use to solve the problems.

Alisha and her dad make a big batch of tomato sauce. They put 4 cups of sauce in each jar, and they fill 6 jars. How many cups of sauce do they make?

The swimming pool holds 8,800 gallons of water. The hot tub holds 500 gallons of water. How much water does it take to fill both?

Review 👤

Color the problems that match the number in the star.

49 ÷ 7
56 ÷ 8
90 ÷ 9

54 ÷ 9
56 ÷ 7
48 ÷ 8

72 ÷ 8
81 ÷ 9
56 ÷ 7

72 ÷ 8
56 ÷ 7
72 ÷ 9

35 ÷ 7
32 ÷ 8
45 ÷ 9

45 ÷ 9
28 ÷ 7
32 ÷ 8

16 ÷ 8
27 ÷ 9
14 ÷ 7

24 ÷ 8
28 ÷ 7
27 ÷ 9

Complete.

6 weeks = ☐ days

4 weeks = ☐ days

☐ weeks = 21 days

☐ weeks = 63 days

950¢ = $ ☐

137¢ = $ ☐

☐ ¢ = $ 2.45

☐ ¢ = $ 7.06

Complete.

40 × 8 = ☐

30 × 9 = ☐

50 × 6 = ☐

80 × 8 = ☐

48 × 2 = ☐

54 × 2 = ☐

64 × 2 = ☐

72 × 2 = ☐

Lesson Activities 👥

A

| milliliter (mL)   1,000 mL = 1 L | liter (L)

B

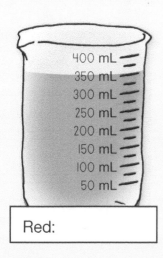

400 mL
350 mL
300 mL
250 mL
200 mL
150 mL
100 mL
50 mL

Red:

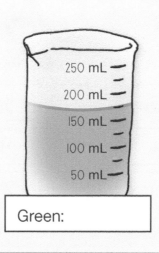

250 mL
200 mL
150 mL
100 mL
50 mL

Green:

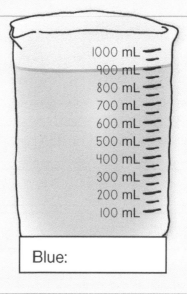

1000 mL
900 mL
800 mL
700 mL
600 mL
500 mL
400 mL
300 mL
200 mL
100 mL

Blue:

C

Capacity Scavenger Hunt

| less than 100 mL | 100-249 mL | 250-499 mL |

| 500-749 mL | 750-999 mL | more than 1 L |

Practice

Choose the more sensible unit for each item.

Capacity of a watering can

8 mL	8 L

Capacity of a soda bottle

2 mL	2 L

Capacity of a medicine bottle

60 mL	60 L

Write how much liquid is in each beaker. Then, use the beakers to answer the questions.

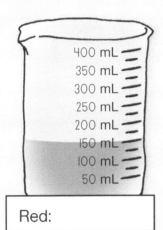

400 mL
350 mL
300 mL
250 mL
200 mL
150 mL
100 mL
50 mL

Red:

250 mL
200 mL
150 mL
100 mL
50 mL

Green:

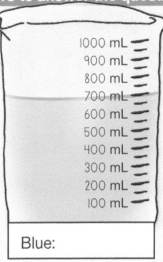

1000 mL
900 mL
800 mL
700 mL
600 mL
500 mL
400 mL
300 mL
200 mL
100 mL

Blue:

How much less red liquid than green liquid is there?

If you pour the red and green liquid into the same beaker, how much liquid will be in the beaker?

If you remove 80 ml of blue liquid from the large beaker, how much liquid will be left?

 If you split the blue liquid equally into 2 beakers, how much liquid will be in each beaker?

Review   Complete.

9	9 0	7	4 9	8	5 6	7	6 3	9	5 4
8	7 2	9	8 1	7	7 0	9	6 3	8	4 8
7	4 2	8	6 4	9	7 2	7	5 6	8	8 0

Complete.

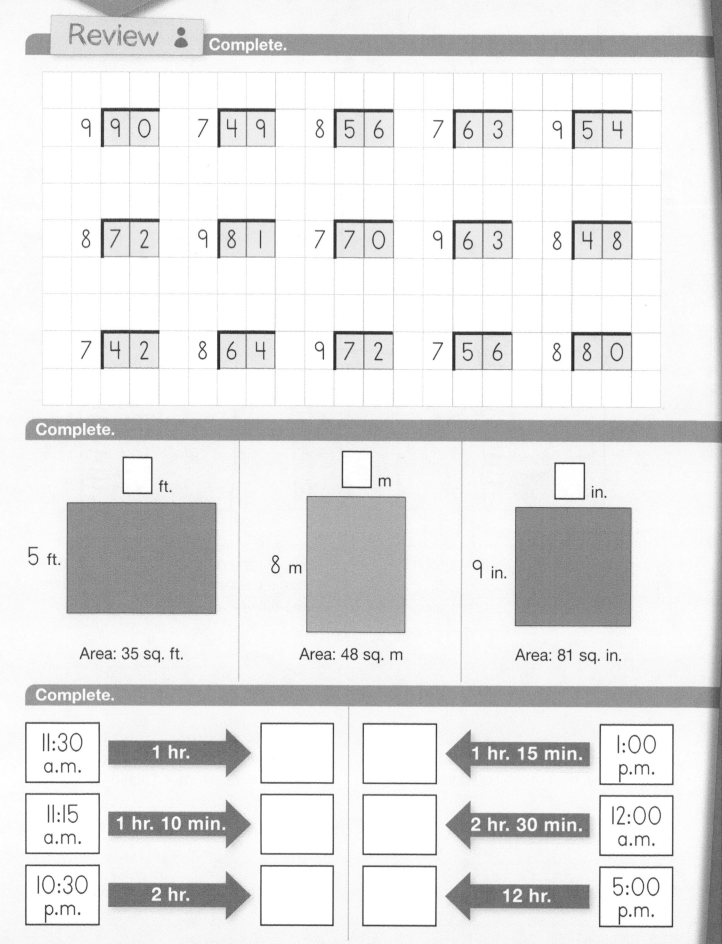

☐ ft.

5 ft.

Area: 35 sq. ft.

☐ m

8 m

Area: 48 sq. m

☐ in.

9 in.

Area: 81 sq. in.

Complete.

11:30 a.m.	→ 1 hr.	☐		☐	← 1 hr. 15 min.	1:00 p.m.
11:15 a.m.	→ 1 hr. 10 min.	☐		☐	← 2 hr. 30 min.	12:00 a.m.
10:30 p.m.	→ 2 hr.	☐		☐	← 12 hr.	5:00 p.m.

Unit Wrap-Up

Choose the more sensible unit for each item.

Weight of a suitcase

| 46 lb. | 46 oz. |

Weight of a purse

| 3 kg | 3 g |

Weight of a wallet

| 100 lb. | 100 g |

Capacity of a bathtub

| 190 L | 190 mL |

Capacity of a wading pool

| 26 gal. | 26 c. |

Capacity of a tea cup

| 1 L | 1 c. |

Capacity of a salad dressing bottle

| 355 mL | 355 qt. |

Weight of a dolphin

| 500 lb. | 500 L |

Capacity of a pitcher

| 2 kg | 2 qt. |

Use the numbers to complete the boxes.

| 2 | 2 | 4 | 16 | 1,000 | 1,000 |

1 lb. = ☐ oz.

1 kg = ☐ g

1 L = ☐ mL

1 pt. = ☐ c.

1 qt. = ☐ pt.

1 gal. = ☐ qt.

16.5

Unit Wrap-Up 👤   Complete. Include the correct units.

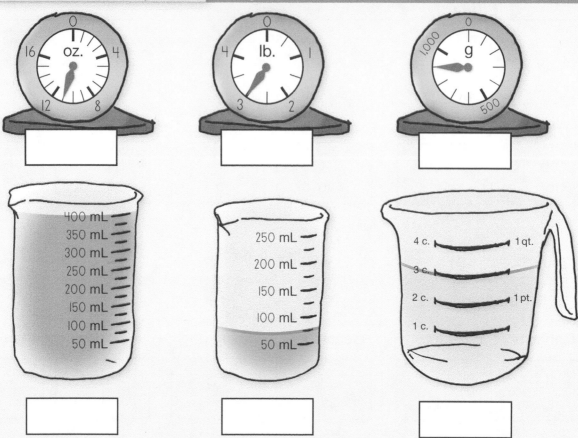

Solve. Write the equations you use to solve the problems.

Sara's guinea pig weighs 890 g. Her hamster weighs 120 g. How much less does her hamster weigh than her guinea pig?

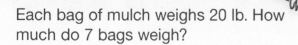

There are 450 mL of water in the water bottle. If you drink 225 mL, how much water is left?

Each bag of mulch weighs 20 lb. How much do 7 bags weigh?

Aman's family fills 6 pitchers with punch for a party. Each pitcher holds 8 cups. How many cups of punch do they have?

Lesson Activities

A

Make Your Own Math Game

Start	+	−	+
			−

+	−	+	
−			
	+	−	+
			−

+	−	+	
−			
	+	−	+
			−

+	−	+	
End			

16.6

Complete.

	5,	4	8	1
+	2,	6	0	9

	4,	2	8	6
−		2,	7	4	5

	5.	5	0
−	3.	6	4
$			

Round to the nearest thousand.

4,960	
8,007	
5,531	
2,399	
788	

Complete.

Expanded Form	Number
700 + 90 + 4	
2,000 + 600 + 8	
	5,902
	4,075

Complete.

$ _____

$ _____

Complete with <, >, or =.

2,000 + 5 ◯ 2,000 + 50

500 + 500 ◯ 700 + 300

4,200 − 400 ◯ 4,300 − 600

580 + 50 ◯ 570 + 60

7,800 + 600 ◯ 7,900 + 500

730 + 80 ◯ 750 + 50

Review ⚬ Complete the sequences.

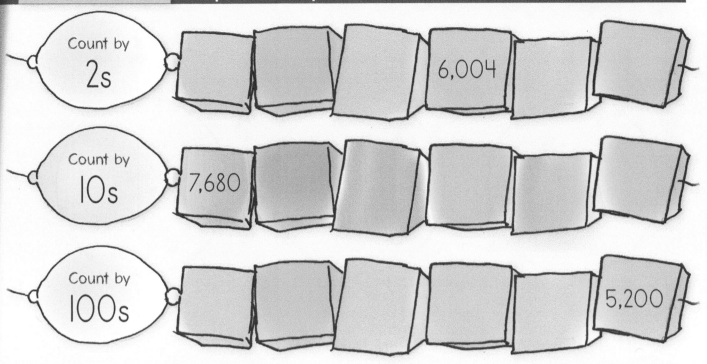

Count by 2s: ___ ___ ___ 6,004 ___ ___

Count by 10s: 7,680 ___ ___ ___ ___ ___

Count by 100s: ___ ___ ___ ___ 5,200

Solve. Write the equations you use to solve the problems.

Mom is 36 years old. Carlos is 28 years younger than Mom. Grandma is 53 years older than Carlos. How old is Grandma?

A cup of cocoa costs $1.79. A muffin costs $1.35 more than cocoa. How much does it cost to buy cocoa and a muffin?

The sum of 3 numbers is 100.
One number is 35. Another number is 15.
What is the last number?

Julia spends $4.25 on a hot dog and $1.50 on a drink. She gives the clerk $10.00. How much change does she get?

Lesson Activities 👥

Multiples of 1

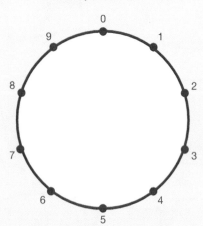

Multiples of 2

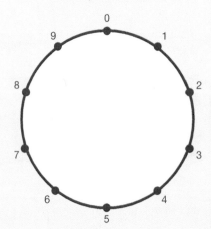

Multiples of 3

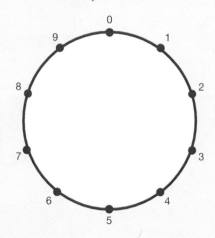

Multiples of 4

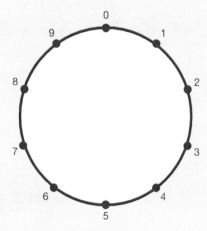

Multiples of 5

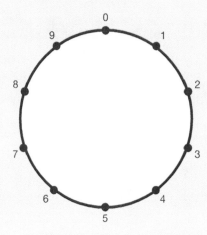

Multiples of 6

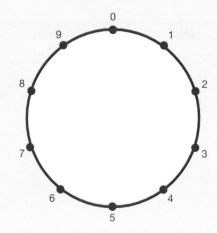

Multiples of 7

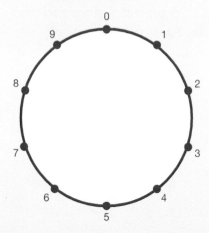

Multiples of 8

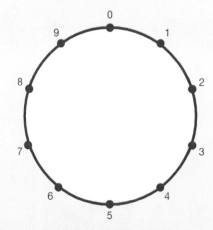

Multiples of 9

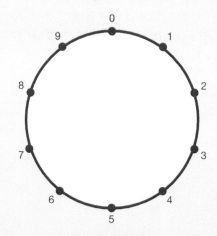

Practice 👤 Complete the fact family to match the array.

☐ × ☐ = ☐

☐ × ☐ = ☐

☐ ÷ ☐ = ☐

☐ ÷ ☐ = ☐

Complete.

4 × 3 = ☐   9 × 6 = ☐   10 × 8 = ☐

7 × 7 = ☐   9 × 8 = ☐   6 × 7 = ☐

4 × 8 = ☐   6 × 4 = ☐   4 × 9 = ☐

8 × 6 = ☐   5 × 10 = ☐   7 × 4 = ☐

5 × 9 = ☐   8 × 7 = ☐   6 × 7 = ☐

Complete.

4 × 8 + 3 = ☐

9 × 6 + 1 = ☐

35 × 2 = ☐

47 × 2 = ☐

90 × 3 = ☐

50 × 6 = ☐

Solve. Write the equations you use.

Ruth earns $9 for mowing the lawn. If she mows the lawn 7 times, how much money will she earn?

16.7

Review   Complete.

18 ÷ 2 = ☐   28 ÷ 7 = ☐   40 ÷ 5 = ☐

36 ÷ 6 = ☐   27 ÷ 3 = ☐   35 ÷ 7 = ☐

54 ÷ 9 = ☐   90 ÷ 10 = ☐   72 ÷ 9 = ☐

48 ÷ 6 = ☐   64 ÷ 8 = ☐   36 ÷ 4 = ☐

49 ÷ 7 = ☐   56 ÷ 8 = ☐   63 ÷ 9 = ☐

Complete. Use long division.

4 ⟌ 3 3   3 ⟌ 2 8   5 ⟌ 4 2

Complete.

☐ ft.

4 ft.

Area: 28 sq. ft.

Solve. Write the equations you use.

Oscar has 38 ft. of string.
He cuts the string into 6-foot-long pieces.
How much string is left over?

Mira's family buys 3 pizzas.
Each pizza has 8 slices. If they eat
17 slices, how many slices are left?

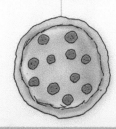

Lesson Activities 👥

in.	lb.	km	sq. mi.
g	sq. yd.	m	sq. ft.
L	oz.	pt.	yd.
cm	ft.	mL	c.
qt.	gal.	sq. cm	min.
sq. km	sq. in.	kg	sq. m
	hr.	mi.	

	U.S.	Metric
Length		
Area		
Weight		
Capacity		
Time		

Practice

Choose the more sensible unit for each item.

Area of a window

1 sq. cm	1 sq. m

Area of a rug

35 sq. in.	35 sq. ft.

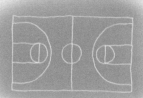

Area of a basketball court

600 sq. yd.	600 sq. mi.

Capacity of a drink can

355 mL	355 L

Capacity of a large pot

3 pt.	3 gal.

Weight of a small dog

9 g	9 kg

Find the perimeter and area.

14 m

7 m

Perimeter:

Area:

5 ft.

3 ft.

4 ft.

6 ft.

3 ft.

9 ft.

Perimeter:

Area:

Solve. Write the equations you use.

The shorter side of the rug is 5 feet long.
The other side is 3 feet longer.
What is the area of the rug?

5 ft.

Cody and his mom use 24 m of fence to enclose this garden. How long is the unlabeled side of the garden?

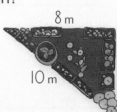

8 m

10 m

Review 👤 **Write the time.**

| : | : | : | : |

Complete the chart.

Start Time	End Time	Elapsed Time
10:30 a.m.	11:15 a.m.	
11:45 a.m.		40 min.
	1:00 p.m.	3 hr.
2:30 p.m.		2 hr. 30 min.
4:45 p.m.	6:20 p.m.	
	12:00 a.m.	1 hr. 50 min.

Solve.

Tim played outside from 11:30 a.m. to 12:20 p.m. How long did he play outside?

Josie starts watching a movie at 6:25 p.m. The movie is 1 hour and 50 minutes long. When will the movie be over?

16.9

Lesson Activities 👥

A

Elements to Include

- Right angle
- Angle larger than a right angle
- Angle smaller than a right angle
- Square
- Rectangle
- Rhombus

B

What was your favorite math activity this year?

What math topic was most interesting to you this year?

What math skill did you work hardest to learn this year?

What do you hope to learn in math next year?

Practice — Complete.

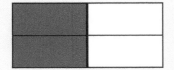
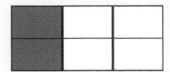

$$\frac{1}{2} = \frac{\boxed{}}{4}$$ $$\frac{1}{3} = \frac{\boxed{}}{6}$$ $$\frac{3}{4} = \frac{\boxed{}}{8}$$

Write <, >, or =.

$$\frac{1}{3} \bigcirc \frac{2}{3}$$

$$\frac{4}{8} \bigcirc \frac{1}{2}$$

$$\frac{2}{3} \bigcirc \frac{2}{8}$$

$$\frac{2}{2} \bigcirc \frac{7}{8}$$

Complete.

$$\frac{4}{8} + \frac{3}{8} = \boxed{}$$

$$\frac{5}{6} - \frac{2}{6} = \boxed{}$$

$$\frac{1}{3} + \frac{2}{3} = \boxed{}$$

$$\frac{4}{4} - \frac{1}{4} = \boxed{}$$

Draw a shape to match each description.

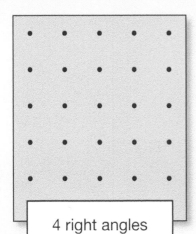

4 right angles

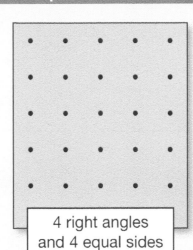

4 right angles
and 4 equal sides

0 right angles
and 4 equal sides

CONGRATULATIONS!

Presented to

_____

for successfully completing

Third Grade Math
with Confidence

_____   _____

Date   Signature